"As I think back to the days of my childhood, the frost-covered windows in my bedroom, the frigid walks to the country school, the excitement of a blizzard, and a hundred other memories, I realize that these experiences left an indelible mark on me and made me who I am today."

The Quiet Season: Remembering Country Winters

A companion to the
Wisconsin Public Television documentary
A FARM WINTER WITH JERRY APPS

The Quiet Season

Remembering Country Winters

Jerry Apps

Wisconsin Historical Society Press

Published by the Wisconsin Historical Society Press
Publishers since 1855

Publication of this book was made possible in part by a grant from the Amy Louise Hunter fellowship fund.

wisconsinhistory.org

Printed in Wisconsin, USA
Cover illustration by John Zimm © 2013
17 16 15 14 13 1 2 3 4 5

Library of Congress Cataloging-in-Publication Data
Apps, Jerold W., 1934–
The quiet season : remembering country winters / Jerry Apps.
pages cm
ISBN 978-0-87020-607-8 (hardcover : alkaline paper) 1. Apps, Jerold W., 1934—Childhood and youth. 2. Apps, Jerold W., 1934—Family. 3. Winter—Wisconsin—History—20th century. 4. Farm life—Wisconsin—History—20th century. 5. Wisconsin—Social life and customs—20th century. 6. Rural families—Wisconsin—History—20th century. 7. Wisconsin—Rural conditions. I. Title.
F586.A65 2013
977.5'043—dc23

2013002122

∞ The paper used in this publication meets the minimum requirements of the American National Standard for Information Sciences—Permanence of Paper for Printed Library Materials, ANSI Z39.48-1992.

"Winter has a concentrated and nutty kernel if you know where to look for it."

—HENRY DAVID THOREAU

journal entry, November 28, 1858

To my brothers, Donald and Darrel, who experienced many of these stories with me, and who have known not quite as many winters as I have.

Introduction

I was born in the midst of the Great Depression and grew up on a central Wisconsin farm, where the winters were fierce and seemingly never ending. I have never left the North, and outside of the time I spent in the army I have never missed a winter in Wisconsin.

Over the years I have come to appreciate and even enjoy northern winters. But I've also learned that there is more to winter than snow and ice and bitter cold. Winter has shaped me in ways that go deeper than I am even aware. I believe this is true for everyone who has spent any length of time in the North. Living through a real winter—a northern winter—affects how we think, influences what we believe is important, and causes us to relate to other people in a particular way.

For farm families like mine, winter meant slowing down. The rest of the year on the farm was near nonstop activity: plowing, stone picking, and planting in spring; cultivating, hoeing, making hay, threshing, and picking cucumbers in summer; silo filling and corn husking in fall. Through it all we also built fence, repaired machinery, tended our animals, and of course milked the cows twice a day. In winter we took a well-earned rest in preparation for the busy seasons to come. The short days and long, dark nights forced us to follow the rhythms of the natural world and reminded us that we were in fact part of nature—not as different from the plants and animals as we might have thought.

There's a resilience that comes with having a few northern Januaries under your belt. Winter on the farm was difficult at best, even dangerous when a blizzard roared in from the northwest and closed us off from the outside world, sometimes for several days. But we never worried about power outages, since we had no outside power; electrical lines would not arrive at our farm until 1947. Our kerosene lamps lit the long evenings, and our wood-burning stoves kept us warm enough. We had no indoor plumbing, either, so we used a gasoline-powered engine to pump water for the farm animals and for our own use. (We also kept our trips to the frigidly cold outhouse as brief as possible.)

Along with a hard-won self-reliance, I credit winter with teaching me the value of patience. It just takes longer to accomplish things in winter. We wallowed through several feet of snow to our woodlot to cut wood for hungry woodstoves, a task slowed considerably by cold weather and deep snow. When snowstorms plugged our road with snowdrifts and stopped all travel past our farm, there was nothing we could do about it except wait for the snowplow, which always came—eventually.

The importance of family came into sharper focus during winter. Although we attended school no matter the weather (our country school never closed), some blizzards kept us from traveling into town for weeks. While those storms made our farmwork all the more challenging—paths had to be cleared from building to building, sometimes several times in one day, and our heavy winter clothing made it that much harder to get our work done—they were also cause for our family to draw closer together. When the weather was especially snowy or bitterly cold, we gathered in the kitchen or the dining room (the only rooms in our farmhouse heated by woodstoves) and played Monopoly, checkers, or card games like Flinch and Smear. My twin brothers and I built things with Tinker Toys and Lincoln Logs and read books that we had brought home from our school library. While we sat at the dining room table to do our homework around the kerosene lantern, our parents joined us, Pa at one end reading the *Milwaukee Sentinel* or the *Wisconsin Agriculturist*, Ma at the other darning socks, mending worn overalls, or working on other sewing projects.

While winter forced us to turn our attention to home and family, it also instilled in us a strong sense of community. In those days farm families relied on each other for all sorts of help, from barn raisings to midwifery. And it was never more important than during winter that we look out for our neighbors, making sure that they were warm and had plenty to eat. Getting caught outside in a blizzard or in below-freezing temperatures can be deadly. Rural people know this very well and tend to keep track of each other during extreme weather.

Besides depending on neighbors for their help with such winter tasks as butchering and sawing wood, we brightened the long winter nights with neighborhood card parties and the occasional dance, sometimes in a neighbor's home, more often at our country school. We celebrated weddings, birthdays, and anniversaries together and likewise came together to mourn the death of a community member. Casseroles, cakes, and pies appeared at the grieving family's home, and everyone attended the funeral, no matter what their religion or whether they were religious at all. Neighbors quickly and quietly showed up to help with the milking and other farm chores during these sad times.

Perhaps most profoundly for me, winter embeds in us northerners a deep respect for the natural world. Nature's power is formidable, never more so than in winter. There's nothing like a blinding blizzard to remind us humans that we are not in charge, even though we sometimes fool ourselves into thinking we are.

Each fresh snowfall provided a canvas for recording recent happenings on the landscape. By learning to identify animal tracks in the snow, a skill I acquired from my father, I could see where a squirrel had dug for acorns, where a deer had pawed for something to eat, where a fox had walked during the previous night. One time I followed a fox trail until I found where it intersected with rabbit tracks. A bit farther along I discovered where the rabbit had met its fate, nothing left but a few drops of blood on the white snow and a few tufts of rabbit fur. The fox track continued on. There on the snow I saw life and death in their simplest terms, a vivid reminder of the natural order of things. My interest in nature and its deeper meaning in our lives has stayed with me since those early experiences. On the snow-swept fields of our farm, I learned a profound lesson about nature as teacher.

This book includes some of my winter stories for the years 1939–1947, the years I attended first through eighth grades at Chain O' Lake Country School. Although winter life on the farm was sometimes miserable, it could also be a fun and glorious time, and here I share both the good and the not-so-good experiences. I also try to capture the hilarious and the serious, the profound and the ordinary, the homely and the beautiful sides of winter. As I think back to the days of my childhood, the frost-covered windows in my bedroom, the frigid walks to the country school, the excitement of a blizzard, and a hundred other memories, I realize that these experiences left an indelible mark on me and made me who I am today.

Preparing for Winter

Some people believe winter arrives on December 21 or 22, depending on what the calendar says that year. But those of us who live in the upper Midwest know better. Here winter arrives as much as a month or so earlier. And while the official vernal equinox is March 20 or 21, it is a rare year that spring comes that early. Once winter arrives in the North, it settles in and is reluctant to leave.

My dad was not much for checking a calendar. As a farmer, he spent his life outdoors, learning to predict the weather by watching sunsets and wind direction and other natural signs. Some of the clues that winter was coming were subtle: the horses' coats grew longer; our farm dog Fanny's hair grew thicker. Others were sure predictors: the last flocks of geese winging their way south over our farm; the oak leaves turning from green to many shades of brown.

To survive winter on the farm required planning and preparation—lots of it. Everyone in the family had jobs to do, starting for my brothers and me when we were only three or four years old. As we got older, more jobs came our way. We spent the summer and fall growing, harvesting, and storing feed for the animals. We filled the haymows in the barn with alfalfa, clover, and timothy hay, filled the silo with corn silage, and shoveled full the grain bins in the granary with freshly threshed oats. The straw stack behind the barn grew ever taller, piled high with threshed oat straw for use as bedding for the animals that would spend long winter days in the barn. We shoveled the corn cribs full to the brim with cob corn that would later be mixed with oats and ground into cattle feed at the local grist mill.

In October we hauled the last of the garden produce into the cellar under the house—the remaining heads of cabbage, the last bushel of carrots, a pile of onions, several squash and pumpkins, and an ample supply of rutabagas. Ma made sure that the cellar shelves were filled with canned vegetables, fruits, jellies, and jams. During the war years, when sugar was rationed and nearly impossible to buy, we grew sweet sorghum, and Ma canned as much as ten gallons of the sweet liquid boiled down to a thick syrup. She would use the sorghum for everything from baking to spreading on pancakes. After the fall butchering, usually in early November, a smoked ham hung on the wall alongside the steps leading to the cellar. In the pantry, just off the kitchen, a huge crock of sauerkraut fermented, offering a reminder of its presence to any visitor to the kitchen.

The late-fall days, often cloudy, sometimes with a cold drizzle or even a daylong cold rain, grew increasingly dreary as daylight hours became shorter. The summer birds—robins and wrens, Baltimore orioles and catbirds, bluebirds and meadowlarks—left for warmer climes. On cool, clear nights we sometimes heard an owl call deep in the woods north of our house, a haunting sound on a dark October evening, when the talk at school was about Halloween and ghosts and goblins. Then, with

Halloween past, winter waited just around the corner like a predator about to leap on its prey.

On a Saturday in late October, we dusted off the wood-burning heater that spent the summer gathering dust in the woodshed and hauled it into the house. The heater was a Round Oak brand, five feet high and half that in diameter, standing on legs that lifted it a foot or so off the floor. It was heavy and clumsy to carry, and Pa asked a couple of the neighbors, usually Bill Miller and Alan Davis, to help with the task. When I was old enough, I got in on that act. We slid two-by-eight planks under the stove and slowly carried the heavy beast across the kitchen floor and into the dining room. There we hefted it onto a metal sheet that would protect the floor. We carefully lined up the stove so the stovepipe would fit through the hole in the dining room ceiling. The stovepipe passed through the upstairs bedroom where my brothers and I slept, providing a hint of heat to our frigid room on its way to the brick chimney gracing the roofline of our house.

With the stove in place, Ma immediately began dusting it, removing the long summer's accumulation of grime, trying to make the old stove look somewhat respectable so any city relatives who might stop by wouldn't make a negative comment. Meanwhile, Pa opened the stove's door, rumpled up some old newspapers, gathered a few sticks of wood from the kitchen wood box, and lit a fire. He wanted to be sure that everything was in working order, especially that the stovepipe was straight and true and that the smoke was going up the chimney and not gathering in the dining room.

"By golly, she's workin'," Pa said, and a smile spread across his face. Ma put out the cookies and coffee she had ready to thank Bill and Alan for their efforts, and the men hung around for an hour or so, talking and swapping stories before they left for their farms and their own late-fall work.

Next in line for winter preparations was banking the house. When our house was built, around 1900, little was known about insulation in house walls. The walls consisted of wood, lath, and plaster—sturdy, but with few insulating qualities. So like most of our neighbors, in late autumn we piled our own version of insulation around the house's fieldstone foundation. First Pa hitched the team to the manure spreader, and my brothers and I forked it full of straw from the straw stack. Next Pa unrolled four-foot-wide black tarpaper and, with a hammer, tacked it along the bottom of the house, all the way around. He used shingle nails and long strips of wooden lath to hold the tarpaper in place. Then we piled straw against the tarpaper, three feet deep or so, hoping to prevent the worst of the winter winds from whistling around our feet. (Some of our neighbors banked their houses with horse manure, claiming that the manure not only kept out the wind but also created some heat. Ma wanted nothing to do with that approach—how would she explain to the city relatives that our house was surrounded by horse manure?)

When we finished banking the house, we covered the front door with a piece of tarpaper to help keep out the drafts. We never used the front door as an entry, anyway, no matter the season, though we did open it on hot summer days to provide ventilation. The screen door in the kitchen was also covered with tarpaper to ward off the cold that seeped into the kitchen on the coldest days.

Pa checked the woodstoves in the pump house and in

the potato cellar to make sure they were in working order. The former kept the pump from freezing and cutting off the water supply for the cattle, horses, and hogs—and for us, although we used very little water during the winter. The latter would not be lit until frost threatened our cash crop of potatoes, usually in mid-November.

Pa dug around in the machine shed and found the water tank heater, a wood-burning stove that kept our outdoor stock tank from freezing. About two-thirds of the stove would be immersed in the water tank; the remaining third, which consisted of a stovepipe and a little door for stuffing wood into the stove, would stick up above the tank's surface. The stock tank received its water from the overflow of the milk-cooling tank in the pump house. In the cold months, when the cattle were housed in the barn twenty-four hours a day, we let them outside once or twice a day to drink from the water tank. The short trip to the water tank provided the cows some exercise, and briefly moving them out of their stanchions made it easier to carry in straw for their bedding.

While Pa was making these preparations, Ma continued to convert the house to winter mode. The double doors to the parlor and the back bedroom that led off of it were closed for the winter. Our family would essentially live in two rooms, the kitchen and the dining room, the only rooms that had wood-burning stoves. Ma and Pa's bedroom, off the dining room, received some heat from the dining room's heater, and my brothers and I made do with the little heat that seeped from the dining room heater's stovepipe.

Now, after much toil, the house was buttoned up and ready for whatever winter would bring our way.

Butchering

Butchering is not for the faint of heart. As long as we humans include meat in our diets, animals will die. As a farm kid, butchering a hog each fall was as natural an event as digging potatoes or cutting cabbage heads from the garden. We needed the meat if we were going to survive the long winter. And to the best of my knowledge, nobody in our neighborhood said one word about the fact that enjoying a pork chop, a thick slice of ham, or some crispy bacon meant that a pig had died.

During the war years, my dad raised sixty or so hogs—Berkshires and Chester Whites—each year. Berkshires are mostly black, with a turned-up nose; Chester Whites are completely white, with long noses. The term *mortgage lifter* was commonly used in those days when raising hogs was mentioned—and it certainly was true in the case of my father, who sent as many as fifty of his hogs to market each fall. The price paid for hogs had risen considerably since the Depression years, and Pa was able to make enough money to pay off the mortgage on the farm before the war ended. He kept the remaining ten or so sows for the next year's hog production, plus a couple of choice barrows (castrated males) for butchering.

Early November was the time for butchering. Pa chose a Saturday, when my brothers and I were home from school, so I could help. Like so many jobs on the farm, butchering involved neighbors working together, and every fall our closest neighbor, Bill Miller, and Pa helped each other with the task.

Hog butchering involved several steps, each important and each requiring a certain amount of skill. While there was little variation in the ritual from year to year, I recall one butchering day in particular. Early that morning Pa started a fire under the big cast-iron kettle in one corner of the pump house and filled the kettle with water. By midmorning, when Bill arrived to help, the water was steaming hot. In the nearby shed, Pa set up the scalding table, which consisted of some planks laid across a pair of sawhorses.

Pa had segregated this year's pig—a Chester White barrow—in a corner of the hog pen away from the others. Pigs could be unpredictable, and keeping the others away from the killing made sure they wouldn't get in the way.

Killing the pig was the easiest part of the process. Pa aimed his .22 rifle between the pig's eyes. One shot, and the pig was down and dead—no suffering. Immediately Bill cut the pig's throat, allowing it to quickly bleed out onto the ground. Some folks, including the Millers, would catch the pig blood in a pan and use it for making blood sausage, but my folks didn't do that.

Next we rolled the carcass onto the stone boat. Pa harnessed Frank and Charlie, our dependable team of Percheron draft horses, to the stone boat so they could pull the carcass to the shed. Luckily, the smell of blood didn't faze the Percherons. One year Pa had hitched Dick, the Western mustang he had bought from a horse dealer, to the stone boat to haul the butchered pig. When Dick smelled the hog's blood, he took off at a gallop, dragging the stone boat with the dead pig behind him. Dick jumped over Pa's new wooden barnyard gate, but the stone boat with the pig did not. The new gate exploded, slivers of wood flying everywhere. The pig rolled off the stone boat and lay in the barnyard while Pa caught Dick and took him back to the barn.

A fifty-five-gallon steel barrel, its top removed, sat in front of the scalding table. Pa, Bill, and I hoisted the dead pig onto the table. Then Pa and Bill began carrying pails of boiling water from the pump house, filling the barrel a bit more than half full. Their next task was to each grasp one of the pig's hind legs and then slide the carcass up and down in the boiling water, back end first, then front end first. This loosened the animal's hair, which Pa and Bill removed with a scraper, a slightly concave circular metal device about six inches in diameter with a short wooden handle. The sharp smell of wet pig hair filled the air. After the hair was removed, the men shoved a gambrel stick through a slit in each of the now naked pig's back legs. About two feet long, the gambrel stick had an eyebolt through it, and here Pa fastened the block and tackle, a series of ropes and pulleys attached to the shed's slanted ceiling. We removed the planks and sawhorses, and Pa pulled the pig upright so that its head hung above the ground. With a sharp butcher knife, Pa made a slit from between the pig's hind legs all the way to its head, exposing the internal organs: heart, intestines, liver, and lungs. As the organs began to sag out of the body cavity, Bill held them in his arms while Pa continued cutting them loose. Pa removed the liver and the heart and placed them in a dish pan that Ma had provided. We did not save the intestines, but some people did clean them and use them for sausage making.

The smell of pig entrails is strong and pungent and different from most every other smell around the farm. It doesn't burn your eyes like chicken manure, or work its way into your wool clothing like cow and hog manure. But it's a smell I've never forgotten.

Bill carried the armful of entrails out to the field past the machine shed and dumped them in a pile. Within a few days the pile would disappear as crows and foxes feasted. With this part of the butchering process complete, we filed into the house for coffee and cookies and a round of storytelling. Bill Miller was known as the best storyteller in the neighborhood; he was also known to make up stories out of whole cloth, so when you listened to him you never knew what was true and what was not. My mother was a stickler for the truth and had no patience for embellished stories. In fact, she referred to Bill Miller (not to his face, of course) as the biggest liar that had ever come down a country road. I didn't much care about what was fact and what was fiction: a good story was a good story. So I always enjoyed Bill's visits. After an hour or so of story swapping (Pa was no slouch at telling a good story, either), Bill grabbed his cap, put on his denim coat, and walked off down the road toward home and his own farmwork.

Pa grabbed the meat saw and the butcher knives, and we headed out to the shed and the naked white pig hanging with its nose just off the frozen ground. "Hold on to its head," Pa instructed. He worked the meat saw back and forth against the pig's neck, severing the head from the rest of the carcass. Soon I was holding an armful of pig head, its eyes still open and blankly staring. I carried it to the house, where Ma was prepared to remove the skin and carve off the meat to make something called headcheese.

Next Pa began sawing between the hind legs and sawed through to the front end of the carcass, creating two halves. We each carried a half pig into the kitchen and laid it on the kitchen table, which was covered with its usual oilcloth. Pa cut off the four feet with the meat saw, and then Ma and Pa, each wielding butcher knives, cut out the bacon bellies, cut off the pork shoulder, and removed the hams. Next they cut the loin, the part of the hog next to the backbone, into pork chops. They wasted no part of the pig, saving even the tail. On Monday Pa would take the bacon bellies and hams to the meat market in Wautoma to be smoked; then they could hang alongside the cellar steps all winter without spoiling.

All the while, Ma cut off any fat she came across, cut it into little squares, and tossed it into a big pan. She put the pan of hog fat on the woodstove to melt, a process she called rendering the lard. After it had melted down a bit, she placed the lard in a lard press (the press could also be used as a cider press, but we never used it for that purpose). As she turned the handle on the top of the press, liquid lard poured out of its spout into big gallon jars. Ma allowed the jars to cool, screwed on covers, and placed the jars on the cellar shelves along with the other canned goods. She would use the lard throughout the year for baking and for frying such things as potatoes and eggs.

That night we enjoyed pork chops for supper, and what a treat they were. I could think of no meat that tasted better than a fresh, thick-cut pork chop—unless it was a thick slice of smoked ham. We'd have to wait a few weeks for the smoked ham. The pork chops we could enjoy right away.

Making Wood

On a cool November Saturday morning, after a breakfast of flapjacks and bacon, Pa made the announcement. "Time to start making wood," he said matter-of-factly as he pushed himself back from the kitchen table. He was looking at me when he said it, and I knew I'd be spending that Saturday in the woods. He hadn't said a word about making wood when my brothers and I got home from school on Friday afternoon, but we had recognized the signals. I had seen his freshly sharpened double-bitted ax standing in the corner of the pump house when I went out for water that evening; next to it stood the two-handled crosscut saw, along with the single-bitted ax that was mine to use in the woods.

"Making wood" meant turning dead oak trees into hunks of wood suitable for keeping the several woodstoves on our farm operating during the long, cold central Wisconsin winter. About twenty acres of oak trees nuzzled up to the north side of our farmstead, so the wood supply was handy. Nonetheless, making wood was hard work and took considerable time. The saying "Chop your own wood and it will warm you twice" was obviously dreamed up by someone who hadn't spent any time actually cutting wood. Making wood offers far more than two opportunities for warming.

With the morning barn chores finished, we "shouldered our axes," as Pa described the proper way to carry what could be a dangerous tool. He carried the crosscut saw with the teeth pointed up. We headed out to the woods, where while squirrel hunting earlier that fall we had spotted several dead oaks—good candidates for the ax and saw.

The ax is one of the oldest human implements. It was a mainstay of the pioneers who settled Wisconsin back in the 1800s and the main tool the loggers used to cut through the vast forests of northern Wisconsin. Pa took good care of his axes and kept them razor sharp. "A sharp tool is a safer tool," he liked to say. A sharp tool also made the work a bit easier, if swinging an ax can ever be considered easy.

We crunched through fallen leaves on our way to the first candidate for cutting, a dead oak with a trunk three feet across and thirty feet tall with dead limbs sticking out every which way. Pa walked around the tree once, determining its natural lean—the direction it would most likely fall. He also looked for trees that might be in the way when the tree fell. The last thing he wanted was a cut tree "hung up" in another tree. A hung-up tree, referred to as a widow-maker, was more than frustrating; it was dangerous. When a tree fell only partway, you never knew when it would fall the rest of the way.

Pa put down the saw, grabbed his double-bitted ax, and took a mighty swing at the tree. *Thwack*. He removed the ax and struck the tree again just to the side of where he had previously cut. *Thwack*. He was notching the tree on the side toward which it should fall—would fall, if his calculations were correct. A pile of wood chips gathered on Pa's six-buckle rubber boots as he continued chopping. Then, with the notching finished, he picked up the saw and instructed me to take one end of it. He ran the saw across the side of the tree opposite from where he had notched, making the first cutting groove. With the groove complete, Pa and I pulled the saw steadily back and forth, back and forth, always pulling, never pushing. If you pushed, the saw pinched. "Let the saw do the work," Pa said. "Don't force it. Work with it."

These were the days before chainsaws made quick work of sawing through a tree. Sawing with a crosscut saw was slow, hard work, but it had its benefits too, the main one being the sweet smell of the oak sawdust that gathered at my feet as I pulled, and pulled again, and pulled once more until I thought my arms would jerk out of their sockets.

Finally, when I thought I couldn't pull the saw one more time, Pa said it was time for a break. He stood up and stretched out his back, and I did the same, for pulling a crosscut saw while bent over not only tested your arms but also challenged your back. After a five-minute break we were back pulling on the saw as it slowly bit its way through the giant oak. The tree continued to stand straight and tall and apparently unfazed by either the chopping or the sawing.

"Not long now," Pa finally said after the saw had made its way through most of the tree and was approaching the notch Pa had made with the ax. And then, with a crack like a rifle shot, the big old oak began toppling, slowly at first and then more rapidly.

"Timber!" Pa yelled. We yanked the saw away from the tree and jumped out of the way as the mighty oak crashed to the ground, the sound of its falling echoing through the quiet woodlot. With the tree down, Pa grabbed the crosscut saw again, and we began cutting the larger limbs off the trunk into pieces about twelve or fourteen feet long. We pulled the pieces off to the side to await loading on our steel-wheeled wagon and hauling to the farmstead, where we'd stack them in a pile. Limbs too small for burning we made into brush piles, "a place for a rabbit to live," Pa said.

During the following week, while my brothers and I were in school, Pa continued cutting trees with the help of Weston Coombes, a neighbor he sometimes hired to help with tasks such as this. With Frank and Charlie, our draft horses, pulling the wagon, Pa and Weston hauled load after load of dead oak trees, sawed into manageable pieces, to the farmstead. When the pile was thirty or so feet long and six to ten feet tall, Pa stopped cutting trees and hauling limbs and trunks to the pile. On Friday evening he began calling neighbors, starting with the sawyer, Guy York, who lived northwest of our farm and owned a circle saw powered by a big Buick engine. Pa asked Guy if he would bring his rig to our farm the next day to saw the enormous pile of oak limbs and tree trunks. Guy said he would. Next Pa called other neighbors to invite them to the sawing bee: Alan Davis, who lived three-quarters of a mile or so straight north of our place, and Bill Miller, who lived a half mile away to the south; George Kolka, who lived a mile west of us; and Danny and Roman Macijeski, a half mile to the east. Pa told them to be at our farm by ten or so on Saturday morning; by then Guy York would have the saw set up and we'd be ready for sawing wood.

Shortly after ten on Saturday, Guy York fired up the old

Buick car engine that he had mounted on the back of a wagon. A belt pulley ran from the engine to the saw frame that sat on the ground near the end of the pile of limbs and tree trunks. The saw, a simple homemade affair, consisted of a large circle saw that ran free without any protection—you learned to stay away from the menacing teeth that cut through dead oak wood like a kitchen knife cuts through a pound of warm butter—and a movable table where you placed the wood to be cut. Once the wood was on the table, York pushed it into the fast-spinning saw, which immediately sliced off a piece. One person took the cut piece and tossed it onto the woodpile. The rest of the crew brought limbs and trunks to the saw, moving rapidly enough so the saw never stopped, except when a set was complete and the saw was moved.

The men moved the circle saw whenever the pile of cut wood became too tall and the distance between the remaining wood to be sawed and the circle saw became too great. That pile was called a "set." The size of a farmer's woodpile was measured by the number of sets. In those days one judged the quality of the neighbor's ambition by the size of his woodpile, among other criteria. The number of sets of wood sawed was an easy way of determining the size of a woodpile.

At noon York shut down the saw, and the crew filed into the house for a feast consisting of mashed potatoes, pork chops or roast beef, Ma's home-canned peas and carrots, two kinds of pie, and several cups of black coffee for each worker. Ma had been busy in the kitchen all morning preparing the meal. Donald and Darrel mostly watched the goings on, helped Ma some in the kitchen, and of course enjoyed the big meal, even though they were stuck eating in the kitchen while the workers, me included, ate in the dining room. After a brief rest the crew was back at work. Usually before dark—and dark came early in late fall—the sawing bee was done. The men filed into the house once more for supper and then made their way home to do their chores. Each farmer in our community would have one or more sawing bees before winter had passed, as each had several hungry woodstoves of their own.

Farm Kitchen

With winter's supply of wood cut and stacked, we could now keep our voracious woodstoves satisfied. Our farm kitchen with its wood-burning cookstove was the heart of our farm, especially in winter. It was in the kitchen that we ate our meals, shared what happened in school, warmed up after a cold round of chores, listened to the radio, and took phone calls on the big wooden party-line telephone that hung on the wall near the outside door. It was in the kitchen that Ma baked bread, cooked meals, and washed and ironed clothes. It was where the Watkins man displayed his products: liniment, salve, pepper, vanilla, and much more. It was where we made big plans for the future and tried to dismiss the disappointments that sometimes came our way.

Our wooden kitchen table, large enough to seat eight people, sat at the center of the room, moved to the side only on wash day to make room for the washing machine and tubs that Pa dragged in from the woodshed. The table was old, scarred, and sturdy; most of the time it was covered with a red-and-black-checked oilcloth. A kerosene lamp stood in the middle of the table every day of the winter months, and many days in spring and fall, too, as the kitchen was at the west side of the house, with limited natural light filtering in through windows on the north and south. A woodshed was attached to the west end of the kitchen, and at the east end a door led to the dining room. The outside door on the south opened onto a roofed but open porch.

Ma kneaded bread on the kitchen table, rolled out cookies, and sewed various items of clothing for us, often out of remnants of cotton feed sacks with designs imprinted on them. It was at the kitchen table that Ma sewed together my first teddy bear. The pattern for the little bear had been printed on a feed sack; Ma cut out the pieces, sewed them together, and stuffed the little bear with cotton batting.

Ma folded clothes on the kitchen table, sat by it to peel potatoes, mended clothes and darned socks there. She studied the Sears, Roebuck catalog at the kitchen table and made out orders for new socks, shirts, and whatever else in the way of clothing had worn out and needed replacing. At the kitchen table she pored over the new seed catalogs when they arrived shortly after the new year. She studied the new varieties carefully but usually ordered those vegetable seeds with which she was familiar and had good success.

Along with the kitchen table, the wood-burning cookstove had a prominent and permanent place in the kitchen, its stovepipe pushed into a brick chimney on the wall behind it. Ma did all of the cooking on the stove, in all seasons of the year. It was cast iron, black with silver trim. The firebox was on the left side of the stove, and a reservoir for warming water was on the right. Six lids sat above the firebox, the hottest of them directly over it on the left. Ma varied the cooking heat for various foods by moving the pots and pans around on the lids. To keep things warm, she placed them far to the right. To bring water to a boil, she moved the pot to the left, the hottest part of the stove. The stove also included a large oven where Ma did all her baking. There were no thermometers, no dials to set; everything was done by feel, sight, and experience. Ma knew which sticks of wood to put in the stove for a quick fire (pine) and which to use for a long, sustaining heat (oak).

Another feature of the stove was a warming oven about two feet above the stove's cooking surface. This was where Ma put sweet rolls to rise, where she kept food warm before serving it, and where she put anything that needed warming but didn't require direct heat.

Woodstoves can be messy and very demanding with their constant requirement for more wood. It seemed to me that Ma was forever asking my brothers or me to haul in wood. And burning wood creates ashes, which had to be removed from the stove every day. By spring a considerable ash pile had formed in the secluded yard just to the north of the kitchen. (With the first warm weather in spring, Pa shoveled the ashes into the manure spreader and spread them on our potato field; wood ashes are a good source of potash, which potatoes need to grow well.) Ma was constantly sweeping up ashes that spilled on the linoleum kitchen floor—and complaining about the dust that seemed to accumulate everywhere in the kitchen. On windy days, occasionally a puff of smoke that was supposed to go up the chimney sneaked out around the stove lids and settled under the kitchen ceiling, over time turning the white ceiling gray.

The fire in the kitchen stove would go out overnight, and

every morning Pa started it up again before he left the house for milking. On below-zero nights the temperature in the kitchen, along with the rest of the house, was well below freezing. Ironically, what we didn't want to freeze solid we kept in the insulated icebox that stood at the north end of the kitchen.

At the back of the stove we hung wet mittens to dry; we hung our wet coats on chairs alongside the stove. On cold nights Pa often rested his feet on the open oven door, the warmest place in the house when the weather was blustery.

The teakettle always sat at a back corner of the cookstove. It wasn't much to look at: dented in several places, dull aluminum in color, with a chipped black handle. But it played an important part in our lives. The teakettle was misnamed; maybe only once or twice during the years I lived at home was water from our teakettle used to make tea, and then only when a persnickety city relative complained that coffee wasn't good for you and insisted on sipping bitter, foul-smelling black tea. With no running water in the house, the teakettle was our main source of hot water. We made many demands on it, especially during the winter. When my brothers or I came down with a sore throat, we gargled with hot water—as hot as we could bear—with a goodly amount of table salt mixed in. When we suffered from colds, a whiskey sling was my mother's preferred treatment. The recipe: start with a glass of hot water, not so hot that it would burn your mouth and throat, but hot enough. Into the glass of hot water dump a jigger of "medicinal" whiskey. It tasted awful, but it worked—sort of. After drinking a whiskey sling, and after Ma rubbed an ample amount of skunk grease on your chest (an odorless, white fat from a dead skunk my uncle trapped), she covered your chest with a square of red flannel pinned to your long underwear. You popped into bed to "sweat out" the cold. It must have worked, because I'm still here.

If you got a chill or had a fever or got kicked by a cow or stepped on by a horse, the hot-water bottle came out of the closet. Ma filled it with hot water from the teakettle, wrapped a towel around it, and you held it on the injured body part or merely snuggled up to it when a little extra warmth was what you needed. (Neither of my parents ever considered putting ice on an injury. In winter, cold was the enemy, and we fought hard to keep it at bay. The idea of holding ice on your knee or your foot was close to ludicrous. Besides, we had no refrigerator and thus no ice cubes—though of course we did have 160 acres of ice and snow blanketing our farm.)

The teakettle's hot water served many other purposes both inside and outside the house: thawing a frozen pump, removing ice from the pig trough, providing warm water for the hogs, removing ice from the kitchen porch stoop. Steaming away on the back of the woodstove, the teakettle added humidity to the kitchen. There are few things as comfortable as sitting around the cookstove on a cold winter day, the teakettle's tongue of steam spilling out of its spout adding a quiet sizzle to the subtle sound of oak wood burning. I remember well the little ditty to be acted out with arm motions: "I'm a little teakettle, small and stout. Here is my handle and here is my spout. When I get all steamed up, hear me shout. Tip me over and pour me out." Today at my farm cabin a teakettle sizzles on the back burner of my woodstove. It is there mainly to add humidity to the dry indoor air, but it also triggers an abundance of memories.

First Snow

It had felt like snow for several days. "Feel it in my bones," Ma said. It was mid-November, and each morning's walk to our country school seemed a bit chillier, and damper, too. The bare oaks alongside our country road stood silent against a slate gray sky. More than a week had passed without sunshine—cold, dreary days and ever longer nights.

As we walked to school on this dreary November morning, my brothers and I watched and wished for snow—a change from the dull browns of late fall, the boring landscape devoid of color or excitement. A few days earlier it had rained; the milk truck and the few cars that passed along our dirt road had created ruts that were now frozen into brown ribbons of hard walking. We hiked along the edges of the road, where the frozen dirt and the dried grasses met and the walking was a bit easier. Pa had suggested that we wear our rubber boots to school; he was that sure it would snow. My brothers and I had protested a bit but did what he said. He was usually right, especially when it came to predicting the weather.

As we topped Millers' Hill, we heard the school bell ringing, a clear tone that echoed through the valley and rolled up the hills and along the country roads leading to the school. The big cast-iron bell hanging in the bell tower on top of the school told us it was 8:30 and reminded us to hurry along if we didn't want to be marked tardy.

We walked into the school a few minutes before nine, the official starting time, and were greeted by Maxine Thompson, our teacher that year. We stashed our lunch buckets (former Karo syrup pails) on the shelf in the school's entryway.

"Might as well keep your coats on," Miss Thompson said. "We're about ready for the flag raising." One of the eighth graders grabbed the thick rope that hung in the entryway and led up to the bell tower and gave it a long pull. *Dong, dong, dong,* the bell responded, and another day at Chain O' Lake School, District Number 4, Town of Rose, Waushara County, Wisconsin, began.

We gathered at the flagpole, where another eighth grader had the duty of snapping the flag to the pole rope and pulling the flag into position at the top of the pole. With the flag in place, we all recited the Pledge of Allegiance before filing back into the school and hanging our coats and caps on hooks in the entryway. I glanced at the sky before going inside. The clouds appeared heavier and thicker, and a stiff breeze had come up from the southwest, from the direction of the lake that was a quarter mile or so down the hill and bore the same name as the school, Chain O' Lake.

Miss Thompson had already started the fire in the big wood-burning stove that stood in the back of the school, and the inside of the building was warm and comfortable as we found our seats and took out our books for the day's lessons. Soon the room was quiet, just the way Miss Thompson liked it, the only sounds the *tick-tock, tick-tock* of the Regulator clock on the north wall, the occasional snapping and crackling of wood burning in the big stove, and the southwest wind rattling the windows. Although tall windows on the north and south ends of the school allowed in as much natural light as possible, the light was murky on this dark fall day, and Miss Thompson flipped on the electric lights. Almost none of us had electricity at home, so we all marveled at how a few lightbulbs strung across the ceiling could turn the dreary room into one that was somewhat cheerful on dark, cloudy days.

I had difficulty concentrating on my lessons; all I could think about was the first snow of the season and how everything would change when it arrived. I thought about all the fun things associated with snow—sledding, skiing, snowball fights—and pushed from my mind snow shoveling, wet mittens, and snow-blocked roads.

I saw the first snowflake about midmorning, a half hour or so before recess. At least, I thought it was a snowflake; it was hard to tell, as the wind kicked up bits of leaves and grass and swirled them around. Then I saw another and another, saw them sticking to the schoolhouse windows before melting and sliding down as raindrops might do, leaving little moisture trails.

At recess time we all burst outside, running like calves let out of the barn for the first time, turning our faces to the sky and feeling the snowflakes on our cheeks, trying to form snowballs—there wasn't enough snow yet—and running around like we were possessed by first snowfall demons. Twenty kids celebrated the first snowfall, first graders to eighth graders all rejoicing together. And then Miss Thompson came outside as well, wearing her thin cotton coat and a head scarf. She held out her hand, caught a snowflake, and smiled.

"Let's play fox and geese," someone yelled, and we all gathered at the now snow-covered softball diamond and watched while a couple of the older kids walked a big circle in the snow, then divided the circle into four parts, like spokes in a wheel with a hub in the center. On this day we would not play anti-I-over, run sheep run, kick the can, pom-pom pull-away, or the other school games we played after softball season ended. It was time to shift from fall to winter games.

To play fox and geese, one person is the fox and the rest are geese. The fox chases the geese, who run around the outside of the circle and sometimes escape to the hub, considered a free zone. But only one person may be in the free zone at a time. The last goose the fox catches becomes the next fox, and the game continues.

Back inside the schoolroom after recess, with rosy cheeks and smiles on our faces, we resumed our studies. At noon we would do it all over again, playing and laughing and celebrating the change in seasons. No matter what the calendar said, for most of us kids that first snow signaled the true beginning of winter.

Fun in the Snow

The excitement of winter's first snow was quickly forgotten as we moved into the routine of winter at Chain O' Lake School. Only a few days after the first snowfall, another one arrived, with more fury and spunk than the first and with more snow, too. This meant someone had to shovel paths to the outhouses, to the pump house and woodshed, to the mailbox nailed on a post at the edge of the country road, and to the flagpole so we could continue our flag-raising ceremony each morning. The flagpole ceremony was canceled only when the temperature dipped below zero, and even then the youngster who had received the great honor of putting up the flag each day continued to do so, below zero or not. On those frigid days the rest of us stayed inside the schoolhouse and pledged our allegiance to the flag while we stood at our desks or, on the coldest mornings, huddled around the woodstove, shivering and trying to get warm.

During recess we played fox and geese, and when we grew bored with that we made gigantic snow forts or decided that flinging snowballs at each other was sufficiently interesting that we spent an entire recess doing that. There were the usual disagreements, of course, most often resulting from someone failing to adhere to the rules of snowball engagement that prohibited hitting a fellow student in the head. This happened regularly, sometimes by accident, but frequently on purpose; a firmly packed snowball to the head was a practical way of settling a disagreement that may have occurred a few days or even weeks previously. Of course the student hit in the head with a snowball usually wailed loudly to let everyone know that the snowball thrower had broken the first rule of civil snowball throwing. Then one of two things happened. If the majority of the students knew about the earlier disagreement and believed that the victim of the snowball to the head had it coming, they merely looked the other way and went on with what they were doing. But if the majority sided with the victim—who usually was an above-average actor, suggesting an injury that was many times worse than the reality of snow trickling down his neck—they grabbed the snowball thrower and washed his face with snow. At this point Miss Thompson usually appeared on the scene. She grabbed both the snowball thrower and the snowball receiver and marched them into the schoolhouse with harsh words for each, and no more recess for the rest of the week.

A simple snowball fight thus taught me something important about rules and punishment. There are rules to be followed, whether written or not, and there are consequences if they are not followed. One level of punishment was meted out by your peers, who quickly judged who was in the wrong and took appropriate action. But that was only the beginning of the punishment, for a greater force usually loomed over incidents like this: the schoolteacher, who always, no exception, had the last word. She didn't usually spend much time trying to untangle who was right and who was wrong. It was far easier to punish both culprits. This provided a powerful example to the other students who may have considered settling some longstanding unhappiness with another student during a snowball fight.

But even our teacher couldn't see *everything* that went on, even though most of us believed she had eyes on both sides of her head. Sometimes kids worked out for themselves what fair play meant and the appropriate (as deemed by the kids) punishment for breaking unspoken but well-known rules.

I found this out during a run-in I had with Clair Jenks. Clair was two or three years ahead of me and considerably bigger than I was; while I was four-foot-something tall, Clair was pushing toward six feet. And although he was mostly a decent kid, he did like to play dirty tricks on his classmates.

As soon as the snow was deep enough, sledding and skiing became the most popular playground activities at Chain O' Lake. Lizzie Hatliff, who owned eighty acres of land surrounding the school (actually seventy-nine acres, as the one acre of school grounds was on her land), didn't mind that we schoolkids used the long hill behind the school for our recess play. Shortly after a major snowfall, we were skiing on Hatliff's Hill. The snow was fast, and the skiing was outstanding. I used homemade skis my Grandfather Witt had made from birch boards that he steamed with a teakettle so he could bend up the front ends. He then carved the turned-up ends to a point, so they closely resembled factory-made skis. He even nailed a strip of leather across each ski to hold my boots in place. Unfortunately, the skis did not have grooves on their bottom sides, so steering was challenging. But steering wasn't a problem on Hatliff's Hill, because after several trips down, the tracks in the snow were well worn, and my homemade skis followed them as a train follows railroad tracks.

On one of my trips down the hill I noticed that Clair Jenks had stayed at the bottom, standing to the side of the ski track. Just before I reached the bottom of the hill, he shoved one of his skis across the path in front of me, causing me to go headfirst into a snowdrift when I struck his outstretched ski. I crawled out of the drift, spitting and sputtering and feeling the cold snow sifting down my back. I found my skis in the drift; they appeared to be in better shape than I was. Clair was pointing at me and laughing. The other kids were watching and wondering what would happen next.

My father had a wicked temper, but he seldom showed it. Only once or twice did I see him in a full rage, and it was not pretty. I inherited his temper but also the wisdom to keep it under control in most situations. I thought what Clair had done was a mean, lowlife trick, but it was his pointing and laughing that set me off. I picked up one of my homemade birch skis, swung it in a big circle, and hit Clair alongside the head. He fell in the snow in a heap. He quickly stood back up, rubbing the place on his head where I had clobbered him. His red face was covered with snow, and he looked like he was going to cry. Just then the school bell rang.

Miss Murty, our teacher that year, quickly noticed that Clair was rubbing his head. She inquired if he'd been hurt during the noon break. I sat petrified at my desk. The other pupils had quickly taken out their work. They listened to the exchange but didn't want any part of what they saw about to happen. Everyone knew what had taken place on the ski hill and why Clair was rubbing his head. I anticipated missing at least a week's worth of recess and noon breaks, and maybe even some time after school.

"Happened at home this morning," Clair said, "when I was doing barn chores."

I breathed a sigh of relief. Now neither Clair nor I had to look forward to Miss Murty's punishment, which I knew would have been severe.

Never again did Clair Jenks stick his ski out in front of me while we skied down Hatliff's hill during noon break. I don't think he tried any of his tricks on other kids at our school after that, either. The bump on the head appeared to have mellowed him, and Clair and I got along fine following that little disagreement on the ski hill. We had settled the problem without the need for the intervention of a higher authority.

Winter Chores

With snow on the ground and daytime temperatures hanging below freezing, Pa declared that winter had officially arrived, even though the calendar indicated it was more than a month away. The routine around the farm was now fully in winter mode.

Now that the cows stayed in the barn every day and night, the barn chores increased by many times over summer chores. Straw had to be toted in from the straw stack, silage tossed down from the silo that stood at the east end of the barn, and hay forked from the haymows above the cows in the barn and then tossed down hay chutes to the cattle mangers below. Pa scattered a ground corn-and-oats mixture in front of the cows each morning and night, the amount based on the amount of milk each cow gave. Dry cows (those that were not milking, awaiting the birth of their next calf) received less ground feed. Every morning the manure gutters behind the cows had to be cleaned, a messy, smelly, but necessary daily task. Pa shoveled the manure into a wheelbarrow; when it was full he pushed it out the barn door and along a wooden plank that he kept clear of snow to the manure pile that grew ever larger in the barnyard in front of the barn.

About once a week Pa filled gunny bags (burlap bags) with

cob corn from the corn crib and cotton grain bags with oats from the granary and packed them in the back of the Plymouth after removing the backseat. New tires were nearly impossible to buy during World War II, so when a tire failed, it was replaced with a used one—Pa had several used tires on hand, as did most everyone else who owned cars during the war years. The old car squatted in back and sputtered a bit with its heavy load, but even with the old tires halfway flat, the Plymouth never failed.

The grist mill was a three-story building located just beyond the dam that corralled the Pine River and formed the Wild Rose Mill Pond. Pa backed up to the unloading platform and dragged the bags of oats and corn out of the Plymouth and onto the wooden platform. The miller, Rodney Murty, a longtime friend of Pa's, greeted him and began pulling the sacks of corn and oats to one of several square holes in the mill's floor. The water in the mill pond powered the mill. Under the mill the water, backed up by the dam, provided sufficient force to spin the blades of a Leffel turbine.

Built of massive twelve-inch by twelve-inch timbers, the grist mill was a building of mystery and wonder. I never got to see the basement, where the actual grinding took place, but when the mill was working, the entire sturdy building shook and shuddered. The line shaft—a metal shaft with various-sized pulleys and belts connected to it—hung from the ceiling on the first floor. As it controlled the line shaft's pulleys and belts, the water-powered turbine drove every aspect of the mill's complicated machinery, from the corn shellers to the elevators that moved the grain from one part of the building to another.

In addition to grinding cow feed for the local farmers, the

mill provided electricity for the village of Wild Rose. Besides driving the mill's grindstones, the turbine powered an electrical generator located in a little brick building just beyond the main mill. Thanks to the mill, the village had electrical power by the early 1900s, many years before the electrical lines were strung to rural communities. Because both grinding of feed and generating electricity depended on water power, the electricity for the village was turned on only in the evening, after dark, and was turned off again promptly at eleven o'clock each night. This allowed a sufficient head of water to build up at the dam to ensure that grinding could go on all day without any loss of waterpower.

After the sacks of cob corn and oats were dumped into the square holes in the mill floor, the empty sacks were stacked by the chute, where they would be filled with the warm, fluffy mixture that appeared a few minutes after the grinding. The earthy smell of the freshly ground grain competed for attention with the loud grinding noises coming from the mill basement and with the shaking and shuddering resulting from the machinery's work. Everything in the mill, including the clothes of the miller, was covered with a fine, white dust, a byproduct of the milling process.

Sometimes we had to wait a half hour or longer as other farmers had their grain ground ahead of ours. On the far side of the mill, a little office had been portioned off from the rest of the structure. It contained a small desk, several chairs, and a wood-burning stove that made the mill office a cozy place to wait. On busy grinding days, several farmers gathered in the mill office to swap stories about their cows, about the weather, and always about the war, as several farmers had sons fighting overseas.

If the wait at the mill was unusually long, we walked across Highway 22 to the Wild Rose cheese factory to visit with cheesemaker Marvin Jones. The cheese factory was always warm on a cold winter day. The smells and sounds were so different from those of the mill, just a few yards away: the smell of cheese being made, of fresh milk and cheese curds; the quiet sound of the paddles moving across the cheese vat, stirring the milk, and the occasional rattle of metal against metal as the cheese curds were removed from the vats and placed in presses where the cheddar cheese would be formed. The cheesemaker always welcomed us and offered us fresh cheese curds, the kind that squeak when you bite into them.

With the sacks of freshly ground corn and oats once more stashed in the back of the Plymouth, we drove home. There we unloaded the sacks in the granary, swept out the back of the Plymouth, and replaced the backseat so my brothers and I would have a place to ride if and when we decided to go someplace—although between the weather and wartime rationing of gas and tires, we traveled infrequently in winter.

That was fine, as our winter chores kept us plenty busy. Every time it snowed, my brothers and I shoveled paths from the house to the pump house, from the pump house to the barn, from the house to the outhouse, from the house to the barn, from the barn to the straw stack, from the barn to the granary, from the granary to the chicken house, from the chicken house to the house, and the biggest shoveling job of all, from the pump house to the road—a path wide enough that the milk truck could drive into our yard to pick up our cans of fresh milk each morning.

Lesser but still important daily chores included collecting the eggs from the chicken house, feeding the chickens, and removing the ashes from the stoves in the house, the potato cellar, and the pump house.

One wintertime chore that seemed both tedious and never ending was splitting wood. The big blocks of wood we cut in the fall had to be split into manageable sizes so they would fit inside the kitchen cookstove. When I was four or five, one of my chores was carrying wood from the woodpile to the kitchen woodshed. As I watched Pa split the wood, he made it look easy. Lift the block of wood onto a large splitting block. Study the block to determine the direction of the grain. If you were good at reading the wood's grain, you could strike the block with the splitting ax in just the right place and it would pop open with little effort. If you misread the grain, the ax blade would stick, and you'd spend the next several minutes trying to extract it from the block—embarrassing if Pa was watching, disgusting if you were working by yourself. (I didn't know then that there was art to this, and that Pa had mastered it only after many years of splitting wood.)

By the time I was ten or eleven, I was splitting wood by myself and trying to remember how Pa did it. Along with learning to read the grain, the key was eye-hand coordination. If your mind told you to strike the block in a particular place and you hit it in a different place—well, lots more practice was necessary. The worst mistake of all was to strike over the block and break the ax handle. I did this several times in my early attempts at wood splitting. Pa didn't say much, just grumbled while he fitted the ax head with a new handle.

Winter added many chores to our daily routine on the farm.

Of course, the season also provided a break from the sunup-to-sundown work of spring, summer, and fall: the planting, weeding, and harvesting. Yet one chore was a constant backdrop to all of our days, twice a day, in every season: milking our small herd of cows and toting the milk to the pump house, where we immersed the cans in the cooling tank (in winter the water in the tank kept the milk from freezing).

As we moved into late November, deer season became the topic of conversation around the supper table, as Pa recalled the many hunts he had experienced. On those wintery November days, whenever neighbor men saw each other the talk generally turned to deer hunting, for nearly everyone in our neighborhood hunted deer. It was a true rite of passage for a kid reaching age twelve. I could hardly wait to become a deer hunter.

Deer Hunting

For our family and for many like us, deer hunting, which always began on the Saturday before Thanksgiving, was almost as important a tradition as the Thanksgiving holiday itself. Whitetail deer hunters clad in red jackets and caps got up in the dark of early morning and headed for the woods with high hopes of bagging a ten-point buck. During the Depression years and all through World War II, we regularly supplemented our diet with wild game, so hunting was more than a sport. In addition to deer, we also hunted rabbits, squirrels, ruffed grouse, pheasants, wild ducks, and Canada geese.

In the fall of 1946, when I was twelve, I bought my first rifle, a .22 Remington bolt action, model 512A, with a magazine that held fifteen long rifle bullets. I ordered it from the Sears, Roebuck catalog and paid twenty-five dollars for it, money I had earned picking potatoes and cucumbers. I had been hunting squirrels and rabbits with my dad's .22 since I was nine or ten, so I knew how to handle a rifle and had become quite a good shot.

One Sunday afternoon Pa helped me sight it in, adjusting the rifle's sights so that when I shot it the bullet would arrive precisely where I intended. Pa's admonition was to make a clean kill so the animal would not suffer. After a half-dozen shots and a little adjusting, my new rifle was ready for hunting. For my twelfth birthday in July I had received a new hunting knife with a six-inch blade and leather scabbard so I could attach it to my belt. Pa showed me how to sharpen it with a sharpening stone so the blade would easily slice a piece of paper or shave the hair from your arm.

That year I became eligible to buy a license to hunt deer, something I had been looking forward to for a long time. Pa was a longtime deer hunter, and as a little kid I had listened in awe to his stories when he returned from a day hunting in the "wilds" of Adams County. Almost every year he brought home a buck to add to our winter meat supply. He hunted with a shotgun then, and he also brought home his spent shell casings and gave them to me—my prize from the hunt. I still remember the smell of gunpowder that lingered in those used 12-gauge shells.

Now that I was twelve I was ready for my first deer hunt. Finally November 16 rolled around, opening day of the 1946 deer hunting season. Several weeks earlier Pa and I had bought our deer hunting licenses at the courthouse in Wautoma. The license amounted to a piece of paper to carry in your pocket and produce if a game warden asked for it; a metal tag to fasten to the antlers of a buck if you were lucky enough to shoot one; and a fancy back tag with a string of numbers that you wore on the back of your red jacket (this was in the days before blaze orange hunting gear).

By this time Pa owned a 30-30 Savage lever-action deer rifle. Bill Miller, our neighbor and Pa's longtime hunting partner, hunted with a 30-30 Marlin lever-action. I couldn't use my new .22 rifle, as the caliber was too small for hunting deer, so Pa told me that I could use his old double-barrel 12-gauge shotgun for my first hunt. Ordinarily a shotgun is used with fine shot for hunting rabbits, pheasants, ducks, and grouse. For deer hunting the law required that you use solid lead bullets, called slugs. I had used some of my savings to buy two boxes of slugs, twelve bullets, which should last for at least two years of hunting.

With a shotgun you do little aiming—you mostly point the weapon at what you intend to hit. But would it be different shooting slugs? I should have shot a couple of my new bullets at a target to find out, but I didn't want to run out of bullets when I was in the field and a big buck was standing in front of me.

Until the early 1950s almost no deer could be found in Waushara County. The nearest deer population roamed the unpopulated areas of Adams County, the county just to the west of Waushara. So that's where Pa and Bill Miller and I would head for my first deer hunting adventure. On that cold and dreary November morning, Pa and I were up at 4 a.m. so that we could do the milking and the other barn chores, eat breakfast, pick up Bill, and be on our way. We wanted to arrive at our hunting spot before first light. As Pa drove the old Plymouth through the darkness, he and Bill chatted about other deer hunting trips, about the bucks they had bagged and the ones they had shot at and missed—equally good stories. I'd heard most of them before, during threshing time, or silo filling, or pig butchering. With each telling, the stories improved. The deer were larger and were shot at greater distances and under ever more trying weather conditions: cold rain, snow, sleet, high winds.

My pa was born in Adams County, and he knew the area well. Our family usually went to Adams County every year when the wild blueberries were ripe and ready for picking. Sometimes we visited the site of the log school that Pa first attended back in the early 1900s. The area where Pa and Bill hunted was but a mile from Pa's birthplace.

Pa parked the Plymouth in an open field, near some deep woods. "This is it," he said as he turned off the motor and climbed out of the car. My first deer hunting adventure was about to start! We each found our guns and loaded them. Pa had instructed me to carry extra shells in my pocket because the double-barrel shotgun held but two bullets, one in each barrel. If I shot those two shells and missed, I would need to have extra bullets handy for reloading the gun. Both Bill's and Pa's rifles held six bullets, so they didn't have to worry about quick reloading.

The sun began to streak the eastern sky, providing enough light to shoot if we spotted a buck. White frost covered the ground. Pa said we should spread out about fifty yards apart and walk slowly through the woods so we could catch glimpses of each other as we moved along, our guns at the ready. We walked for ten minutes, then stood absolutely still for up to a half hour, then walked some more. Walk and stand . . . walk and stand. The woods smelled of late fall, decaying leaves mixed with the scent of jack pine that grew abundantly among the oaks. When I got cold from standing—Pa must have gotten cold as well—he signaled for us to move again.

Each step I made was the ultimate in expectancy. I walked with one finger outside the trigger guard and my thumb ready to pull back one of the hammers on the shotgun, a necessary step before pulling the trigger. I walked through hazel brush and black raspberry bushes that tore at my clothing and scratched my hands. I walked around a huge white pine blown down by a summer windstorm. All the while I kept an eye out for Bill and Pa, who walked on either side of me, and for the buck I hoped would appear before me. We walked and waited all morning and saw nothing—not so much as a deer's white tail disappearing in front of us.

"Time to eat our sandwiches," Pa said when twelve o'clock rolled around. I was hungry as could be; it had been a long time since breakfast.

"This afternoon we'll drive over to that high ground near the Roche-a-Cri," Pa said as we ate. He was referring to the Roche-a-Cri River, which snakes its way through this part of Adams County. With our brief lunch break finished, we unloaded and cased our guns and drove the few miles to the river. Slowly Pa maneuvered the Plymouth across the wooden bridge that spanned the river, then up a steep grade to a little field where we parked the car and once more prepared to hunt. "Let's hope we have better luck on this side of the river," he said.

"Can't be any worse than this morning," Bill said as he uncased his Marlin and loaded it.

"Tell you what," Pa said. "Let's do things a little different this afternoon. Jerry and I will make a little drive through these woods. Bill, you walk down to that crossroad." He pointed down the road about a half mile. "You watch for what we kick out. If there's a deer in there, we'll move him your way." This patch of woods was less brushy than where we had been that morning, which meant Pa and I could walk a hundred yards or so apart and still see each other.

I had never driven deer before, so I followed Pa's lead. Every few yards or so, he would yell, "Arr-roop, arr-roop." When we began the drive, Pa said I should try different ways of yelling, making sure each yell was loud enough to be heard at least a half mile on a windless day. As I walked along, I practiced several yells. One sounded something like a dog. Another sounded like I was driving cattle, a version of "Hi-yah!" After a few tries at various calls, I settled on a version of Pa's "arr-roop," which was fairly easy to do and at the same time could be yelled loudly enough to be heard at some distance. I was discovering that driving deer, like so much of deer hunting, was more art than skill (not to mention the considerable luck that had to be involved).

The purpose of a deer drive, of course, is to shake loose any deer that may have bedded down in the area and send them in the direction of a hunter with a rifle. As I walked along, I concentrated on my yelling, varying the volume and trying to walk and yell at the same time and not run out of breath. I had just let out what I considered my best rendition of "arr-roop" when I glimpsed something under a big oak tree. I immediately stopped walking and yelling and concentrated on the movement, thinking it must be a squirrel, or perhaps a grouse. I strained my eyes in the direction of the movement. At first I saw nothing but a floor of fallen leaves and the grayish black trunks of oak trees. Then I caught the movement again and focused on a pair of ears flicking. I immediately thought *jackrabbit*, as the area was known for them. Then I spotted another set of big ears and followed the ears down to heads. Two deer, a buck and a doe, lay in the dead leaves, their ears twitching back and forth. The buck had a big rack of antlers, bigger than any I'd seen Pa bring home from the woods.

It was the first time I had ever seen deer in the wild. My

hands immediately began to shake. My heart was pounding so loudly I was sure the deer could hear it, but they didn't move. I didn't realize it at the time, but the little breeze I had been facing was pushing my scent away from them. I eased behind a big oak and pulled back the hammer on the shotgun. But then I wondered if it was legal to shoot a deer lying down. Pa had never done that, at least he never said he had, probably because he'd never been as lucky as I was now with two deer, one of them a big buck, resting no more than fifty or sixty feet from me.

As I raised the gun to aim, it occurred to me that Pa had never said where to aim when a deer wasn't standing. He had told me to aim just behind the front shoulder, so the bullet would strike the animal's heart and result in an instant kill, with no suffering. But I couldn't see either deer's shoulder; all I could see were antlers, ears, and a sliver of neck.

I aimed the heavy shotgun at the buck's neck, realizing that the barrel was jerking up and down because of my nervousness. Then I remembered Pa saying to take a deep breath, let it out slowly, and then squeeze the trigger. If you *pull* the trigger, Pa said, the gun will jerk sideways and you'll surely miss.

Kaboom, roared the shotgun. The stock slammed into my shoulder like someone had hit me with a sledgehammer. I stumbled backward a couple of steps but didn't fall. My ears were ringing and my hands were shaking, and through the gun smoke I peered toward my target. With the roar of the gun, both deer jumped to their feet, glanced briefly in my direction, and bounded off with giant leaps, their white tails waving. I had missed my target completely.

I flipped open the double barrel, ejected the spent cartridge and replaced it with another from my pocket. What would I tell Bill and Pa? I returned to yelling and walking, hoping I'd run into another buck resting near an oak tree and have another chance. (After more than sixty years of deer hunting I have yet to run into another deer resting in a bed of oak leaves within easy range.)

I emerged from the woods and spotted Bill nearby. I asked him if he'd seen anything come out of the woods.

"I saw a buck and a doe come out way down there," he said, pointing toward a little opening in the trees. "They were on a tear. I didn't have a chance to shoot before they disappeared."

"Oh," I managed to say in response.

"Was it you that shot?" Bill asked.

"It was," I said proudly. "I saw that big buck a-bounding through the woods. I fired once, but he was too far away for a decent shot." I decided then and there that no one, not even Pa, needed to know the real story.

On my first day of deer hunting, I learned a lot about hunting. I also learned what to share about the hunt, and what not to share. It would have been better if I had bagged the buck and added some winter meat to our dinner table, but sometimes a good story is even better than a slab of venison steak—at least, that's what I still tell myself after many years of deer hunting.

THANKSGIVING

As November came to a close, we looked forward to the holiday season, a time for storytelling and feasting. Chores would still need tending to, of course, but soon we would pause, however briefly, to gather around the table with family and celebrate the harvest season just past.

Our extended family took turns hosting Thanksgiving dinner. Sometimes we had Thanksgiving dinner at home, surrounded by aunts and uncles and cousins. Other times we traveled to a relative's home for the celebration. One Thanksgiving dinner that is forever embedded in my memory took place at my Aunt Louise and Uncle Roy's farm, east of Wild Rose. Aunt Louise was my mother's older sister, and when she put on a meal—especially a Thanksgiving meal—she wanted everything to be just right. She and Roy had no children, so according to my mother Aunt Louise had the time "to put on the dog," a phrase country folk used to describe an occasion just a tad finer than what was ordinarily expected. She brought out her good dishes, her finest tablecloth, her "only for company" silverware. She worked for several days baking pies and breads and planning a menu that would be both memorable and hard to top (it seemed sisters sometimes found it necessary to compete with each other, especially when it came to entertaining and, even more importantly, cooking and baking).

It was about a half-hour drive to Aunt Louise and Uncle Roy's farm, so at about eleven o'clock that morning we all piled into the Plymouth and made our way along the sandy country road that snaked through swampland and then topped the little hill where their farm buildings were situated.

I could never tell if Uncle Roy liked kids or not. I suspected he didn't, because he mostly ignored my brothers and me. But we enjoyed just looking at him, because he had the biggest ears we'd ever seen. They seemed to start somewhere near the top of his head and continued on down halfway to his shoulders. I figured that if those ears could flap, Uncle Roy could fly.

We arrived at their farm around 11:30, which gave my brothers and me a chance to nose around the farm a bit before the noon meal. As we got out of the car, Uncle Roy's big yellow mongrel dog, Ralph, greeted us. He was as friendly as a dog could be. His tail wagged as he pushed close to Ma with the hope of a little petting. But Ma didn't like Ralph. She pushed him away, so he walked over to us boys, and we petted him enthusiastically.

Before we set out on our tour of the farm, Ma warned, "Don't you boys get dirty, now. Remember, you're wearing your good clothes." We'd heard that admonition many times, but it never prevented us from doing a little exploring. Uncle Roy didn't have much in the way of buildings: an ordinary little barn that housed his skinny Guernseys, a granary, a corncrib, a pump house, and a shed. After peeking in the barn—nothing interesting there but a cat that skittered off when we pushed open the creaky door—

we checked the corncrib. It was only half full, which meant Roy had had a poor corn crop this year. Then we trekked over to the car shed, where Uncle Roy and Aunt Louise kept their green 1928 Chevrolet. It looked brand-new. What really amazed me was its beautiful wooden steering wheel. I didn't know what our Plymouth's steering wheel was made of, but it sure wasn't wood.

I was sitting in the Chevrolet turning the steering wheel and pretending to drive when Ma called us to dinner. We filed into the house and took the places that Aunt Louise pointed out to us. Uncle Roy sat facing a window that looked out on a little field in front of the house. Ma and Pa sat on the opposite side of the table with Donald between them—they had long ago learned never to put Donald and Darrel together at a table. Aunt Louise sat on a chair nearest the kitchen, and Darrel and I sat next to Uncle Roy.

Oh, the smells in that room! Freshly baked bread, steaming mashed potatoes, a huge bowl of yellow squash, another of home-canned peas and carrots, a bowl of tiny little onions swimming in a scrumptious sauce, a fancy glass dish of homemade dill pickles. And a huge platter of roast turkey. Aunt Louise also had fancy water glasses, filled and sitting in front of each of us.

After a brief prayer, we dug in, trying to remember Ma's earlier warning that we should eat like young gentlemen and not spill anything on Aunt Louise's tablecloth.

When everything had been passed and our plates were heaped with the special foods of Thanksgiving, everyone was quiet, busy pushing food into our mouths. And then it happened. No one saw it coming.

Uncle Roy—who had said nothing since we sat down other than a few mumbled words of grace—yelled at the top of his voice, "RALPH!" Clearly he had spotted his dog committing some unforgivable deed.

Donald jumped at the outburst and spilled his water glass. Water began seeping across the fancy tablecloth, turning it a soppy gray. I bumped my plate, knocking a slab of turkey onto the tablecloth in front of me. Pa dropped a huge hunk of freshly buttered bread on the table. Darrel spilled a spoonful of carrots and peas he'd been dishing up, missing his plate by several inches. Aunt Louise asked, "Good God, Roy, what is it?" Ma looked like she was in pain as she surveyed spilled food everywhere. Darrel and I began chuckling. Donald didn't know if he should bolt for the door or take the consequences of the spilled water. Pa just sat quietly, smiling broadly.

Ma and Aunt Louise scraped up the spilled food. Cloth napkins soaked up the water. Soon we were back to eating as if nothing had happened. I never did find out what Ralph had done to evoke such a loud response from his owner. But of all the Thanksgivings we celebrated during my growing-up years, the one at Uncle Roy and Aunt Louise's farm is the one that my brothers and I remember most vividly. It was only a couple of years after that memorable dinner that we got word that Uncle Roy had died. My brothers and I missed him. I suspect Ralph did, too.

Christmas Is Coming

It truly was a wish book. Starting the week after Thanksgiving, my brothers and I waited impatiently for its arrival in our rural mailbox: the Sears, Roebuck Christmas catalog. There was no other book like it, especially for farm kids who lived miles from a city and had never been in a department store.

The Christmas catalog contained page after page of toys, everything from Lincoln Logs and Tinker Toys to dolls, books, BB guns, and board games of every type. Of course, the catalog also contained clothes for kids and adults, shoes, boots, plus other excellent gifts such as jewelry, radios, and musical instruments—just about anything anyone would want or need. My brothers and I took turns paging through the catalog, making our choices for Christmas presents—what we hoped Santa would bring. My mother said we could pick out one toy and one practical thing, such as a sweater, a pair of mittens, or maybe a winter cap with fancy ear flaps.

As an early lover of books, I remember well the year that I chose *Fun for Boys*, edited by William Allan Brooks. It was 1943, and we were in the depths of World War II. After reading the brief description, "The complete book of games, hobbies, sports and recreation," I knew this was the book for me. The description in the catalog promised that readers would learn how to throw their voices, identify German airplanes, and develop their muscles. I was interested in all of these things, especially how to identify German warplanes. I worried that a German plane might fly over our farm—a Messerschmitt ME 109, for instance—and I wanted to be prepared to identify it.

I also picked out a sweater, a blue one because Ma said I looked good in blue. I really didn't care what color the sweater was as long it wasn't pink or light green or some other girly color. It wasn't the sweater that interested me, anyway; it was the book.

Once we had informed Ma of what we wanted from the Sears Christmas catalog, we turned our attention to other things. After the brief Thanksgiving break we were back at school, working on our numbers, practicing our reading, memorizing our spelling lessons, studying geography, and when we had a free moment, trying to mimic the Spencerian script handwriting that was strung out above the blackboard. (In my case it was hopeless; my handwriting was doomed to resemble chicken scratching more than it would ever come close to what that famous calligrapher, Mr. Spencer, had suggested as a model for all country school children.) Those of us in second grade and above knew that starting that afternoon, for about an hour before the end of every school day, schoolwork would be temporarily pushed aside and we would begin preparing for the Christmas program.

For most people in the Chain O' Lake school district (those residing within two miles in all directions from the school), the Christmas program was the social event of the year. It was an opportunity for parents to see their children perform, a chance for those without children to experience a night out, and a time for everyone in the community to leave behind the troubles and worries of the Depression and the war, at least for one night.

Some country school teachers dreaded the annual Christmas program as much as they looked forward to it. It was common knowledge that some teachers' contracts had not been renewed when their school's Christmas program had been inferior. On the other hand, the program provided a break in the daily routine of school, and more importantly it gave students the chance to explore a new dimension of their education: performing in front of a group.

Many of the pupils attending Chain O' Lake Country School were shy farm kids. I was even shyer than most. If a visitor drove into our farmyard, I was more likely to run and hide than to meet whoever came visiting. The Christmas program helped a roomful of shy kids come out of their shells, at least for one evening.

Around three o'clock on the Monday after Thanksgiving vacation, Miss Murty opened her desk drawer and pulled out a pile of papers. I recognized them as the Christmas program papers: the skits, songs, and recitations that were the backbone of the annual event. She obviously had already spent considerable time planning this year's program. There were no tryouts for various parts in the skits, no choice as to which recitation we each might do, and no opportunity to choose which songs we would sing. Miss Murty had it all figured out, and in the next hour we each would learn what we were expected to do on the Friday night before Christmas break.

Before she handed out the assignments, she talked about the importance of the Christmas program, reminding us how much everyone in the community looked forward to it and how important it was to cheer people up during a time when there wasn't much to cheer about. I wasn't sure what she was trying to say; I was mostly worried about what I would be expected to do. I remembered the year before, how scared I had felt as a first grader, standing on the stage and trying to remember my lines when all I could see was a roomful of people staring at me, waiting for me to mess up—I was sure of that. But I had showed them. I hadn't forgotten my part. It was some kind of Christmas miracle, I guessed.

Miss Murty went on, talking about the importance of the nativity scene, explaining that in many ways it was the core of the entire Christmas program. She told us that for this year she had selected Jim Steinke and Geraldine Hudziak, older students, for the roles of Joseph and Mary. I wondered what I would say if a few Christmas programs from now the teacher asked *me* to play the part of Joseph. I didn't want anything to do with that. How dumb it would be to walk across the stage wearing a bathrobe with a kitchen towel tied around your head, with Mary at your side wearing a bed sheet over her shoulders and a white towel on her head! If I ever had to play that role, I wouldn't hear the end of it from my school buddies. But that possibility was several years off. Right now I had to worry about what I was expected to do this year.

Finally Miss Murty gave the rest of us our assignments. Mine were a short recitation about the importance of Christmas, singing parts in three songs, and a minor role in a skit where we would each hold up a letter that together spelled *Christmas*. After reading through them, I put the papers in my book bag to take home. I knew my mother would be interested in what I would be doing.

Indeed, Ma was more interested in my Christmas program assignments than I was. Together we looked over the sheets of paper, Ma smiling from time to time. Finally she said, "You'll have fun doing this." I, on the other hand, saw the program as a bunch more work to do, stuff to memorize and practice, when I would rather have my nose in a book. By second grade I wanted to spend as much time reading as I could, and memorizing stuff for the Christmas program didn't seem all that important.

Miss Murty thought it was important, though, and she let us know that the next day and every day leading up to the night of the program. Before every practice she gave a little spiel about the importance of the program. And she didn't let up on us until we had every bit of the program down pat.

Two weeks before the performance, the three-member school board spent the better part of a Saturday afternoon putting up the stage. At the front of our schoolroom, they pushed aside the teacher's desk and recitation table. In their place they laid out roughly a dozen two-by-eight-inch planks, nearly as long as the schoolhouse was wide, and nailed them to sawhorses. By chore time that afternoon, the stage was complete. It stood about two feet above the schoolhouse floor, high enough so all the performers could be easily seen from every seat in the room. A length of wire ran from one side of the room to the other, just above the front edge of the stage, and brown stage curtains, stored in the piano bench the rest of the year, were now strung on the wire. The side curtains consisted of bed sheets donated by one of the school board members. On the floor to the left of the stage stood a tall spruce tree waiting to be decorated.

When we arrived at school the next Monday, we were immediately aware that preparations and practice for the Christmas program had ratcheted up several notches. We had been practicing for about an hour at the end of each school day, but this week Miss Murty extended practice time. Now we would spend an hour and a half singing songs like "Up on the House Top" and "Away in the Manger" and trying to keep from giggling when "Mary" and "Joseph" shuffled across the stage in their efforts not to trip on a too-long bathrobe and oversized bed sheet. We also devoted time to decorating the tree with handmade paper snowflakes, bells, and trees and strings of popcorn. There would be no electric lights on the tree, of course.

Excitement mounted as the evening of the program loomed ever closer. On the afternoon of performance day, Miss Murty sent us all home an hour early. "Rest up a little," she said. But I knew I couldn't rest. I was too excited and worried about flubbing my lines or, even worse, completely forgetting what I was supposed to say.

We milked the cows a little early that evening, and Ma brought out a new pair of overalls and shirt that she had ordered from the Sears catalog especially for this night. "I want you to look nice up there on the stage," she told me.

When we arrived at the school, cars were parked along both sides of the road, and the schoolroom was already nearly filled with people. Two gasoline lamps provided light, one at the front of the room and one at the back.

I don't remember much about the program itself, which

means I must have remembered my lines and stayed mainly in tune when I sang Christmas songs with my fellow students. I do remember the skit in which we held the letters spelling *Christmas;* I think it was Clair Jenks who held the letter M upside down so the word came out *Christwas,* evoking chuckles from the audience. Off to the side Miss Murty motioned for him to turn the letter in the right direction, but he never did.

What I remember even more vividly are the Christmas gifts we received after the end of the program. The teacher had put a present for each of us under the Christmas tree, practical items such as handkerchiefs, pencils, and combs. Suddenly, Santa barged into the schoolroom with a hearty "Merry Christmas," stomping the snow from his feet as he moved toward the stage. Some of the babies in the crowd began to howl, frightened out of their wits by this strange character all dressed in red and with an enormous fake white beard. But my classmates and I had been eagerly anticipating Santa's arrival, and we sat at the edge of the stage awaiting our gifts from Miss Murty, which Santa handed out to each of us. The bearded gentleman also gave Miss Murty the presents we kids had brought for her: a scarf, perfume, or hand-knit mittens. Then Santa seemed surprised to find two more presents under the tree.

"Well, what do we have here? Why, this one's for Bill Miller," he said, holding up the present for Bill to retrieve. "And this one is for Herman Apps," he said next, offering a gift to my dad. It had become a custom for a few "unusual" presents to be distributed each year, and both Bill and my dad looked suspicious as they opened theirs. Bill fumbled with the wrapping on a rather long and narrow present and then held up his gift: a real pig's tail.

Everyone laughed and clapped as Bill stood with a silly grin on his face, wondering who in the neighborhood had recently butchered. Of course, the pig tail had come from one of our pigs, the very one that Bill had helped butcher not many weeks before.

Pa opened his present slowly and carefully. He tore off the wrapping paper to reveal a matchbox. When he slid it open, a live and very unhappy English sparrow flew out and fluttered around the ceiling of the schoolroom. More laughter and clapping ensued.

As everyone filed out the door of the school, Pa and a couple of school board members armed with brooms and a mop worked to encourage the angry sparrow to leave the building. It was another Christmas program that would be long remembered.

THE REAL MEANING OF CHRISTMAS

With the school Christmas program behind us and winter break from school about to begin, our thoughts turned to Christmas at home. In one corner of a field on the west side of the farm, Pa had planted some pine trees to keep the wind from eroding this sandy piece of ground. On the weekend before Christmas, Pa, my brothers, and I hiked out to the pine patch to search for just the right tree. When we came to some agreement (never a complete agreement, as my brothers and I had different ideas about what makes a decent Christmas tree), Pa cut one down with his ax. He allowed just so much bickering among the three of us before he made the final decision.

We dragged the tree home and placed it in its base in the dining room. There it would stand, filling the room with its woodsy fragrance, until an evening a couple of days before Christmas when we would decorate it. We had no electric lights, of course, and Pa would have nothing to do with lighted candles on the tree; he thought it preposterous that anyone would consider bringing an open flame anywhere near a tree. Over the years Ma had collected ornaments of various shapes and colors, and we hung them on the tree—very carefully, for if we dropped one it would shatter into a hundred pieces. And although Ma would never say anything if one broke, you could see the hurt in her eyes. Then Pa placed the star on the top of the tree, and the job was finished. While we stood there admiring the decorated tree, Ma made popcorn on the kitchen woodstove. It was a fun evening and a rare opportunity for the entire family to be involved in something together.

After the barn chores on Christmas Eve, we gathered around the table for a supper of oyster stew, something Ma made just once a year. Both my parents remembered eating oyster stew on Christmas Eve as children, and they passed the tradition on to us. The Wild Rose Meat Market carried fresh oysters just once a year, and Ma always bought some on her regular Saturday shopping trip the week before Christmas. As kids we thought fresh oysters looked like something best tossed out for some animal to find. But when they were properly prepared, we found their taste quite agreeable.

Ma served her stew with little round oyster crackers, freshly baked bread, and lots of butter. The stew had a distinct, not-quite-fishy smell, vastly different from Ma's vegetable soup with its blended aromas of tomato, potato, peas, and carrots. Here is the recipe she used—and the one my family still makes on Christmas Eve.

Ma's Oyster Stew

1 pint fresh oysters
1 quart whole milk
1 tablespoon butter
1 teaspoon salt
1/4 teaspoon pepper

In a small pan, cook oysters over medium heat
in the liquid they come in, stirring constantly,
until the oysters' edges curl.

Heat milk in a large pan on low heat.
Add butter and stir until melted.

Add the oysters and liquid to the milk.
Add salt and pepper and heat thoroughly.

Serves 4 people.

After supper Pa and I adjourned to the barn for the evening milking. We did this a bit earlier than usual so our family could attend Christmas Eve services at West Holden Lutheran Church a few miles from our farm. West Holden Lutheran was a mostly Norwegian congregation with a few of us Germans tossed in because we didn't yet have a German Lutheran Church. The church was heated with a big woodstove that stood in the back. It was cozy warm in the back of the church, a little cooler in the pews toward the front. The altar was elaborately decorated with carved wood and an enormous figure of Christ on the cross looking down on the crowd.

The congregation was made up mainly of farm people, although a few Norwegians from the village of Wild Rose attended as well. We were all dressed about the same—nothing fancy, as the Depression hadn't yet run its course and nobody had money to spend on fancy clothes. Still, I noticed sitting in the pew in front of me a woman who wore a coat with a fur collar and had a natty little hat perched on her head. She was clearly "not from around here."

On that chilly Christmas Eve, the old woodstove in the back of the church was having trouble keeping up with the falling temperatures. Each time a church official opened the stove door to shove in another block of wood, a little puff of wood smoke sneaked into the room. I liked the smell of wood smoke; it had a homey smell and always made me feel warm.

Reverend Vevle, a kindly pastor whom our family enjoyed and respected even though he was Norwegian Lutheran, was in the midst of his Christmas Eve sermon. I was dozing, not paying much attention to his words, as the warmth of the stove and aroma of wood smoke drifted around the pew where we sat. I could see that Pa was nodding as well (Ma would soon give him a poke with her elbow). My younger brothers were as usual antagonizing each other—and getting away with it, as Ma was more concerned about Pa going to sleep than the boys' antics.

Just then the fancy-dressed woman sneezed—not a feminine, sniffly kind of sneeze, but a room-filling eruption of noise. I jumped, Pa sat up straight, my brothers began giggling, and Pastor Vevle, with ever so slight a grin on his face, lumbered on with his message of peace on earth, good will toward men.

She sneezed again, and again, and once more. All the kids in the room were now giggling. The finely dressed woman, now with a frilly handkerchief held to her nose, got up from her seat and under her breath muttered, "I'm allergic to wood smoke." She headed for the door in the back of the church, sneezing every step of the way. All heads turned to watch her as she gave one last gigantic sneeze, blew her nose loudly, pushed opened the church door, and walked into the night.

We never saw her again. No one seemed to know where she had come from, and no one knew where she had gone. But for weeks, whenever my twin brothers walked by one of the woodstoves in our house, they uttered the now famous words, "I'm allergic to wood smoke. Achoo! Achoo!"

The next morning, when we had finished milking and had eaten breakfast, we looked for our presents under the Christmas tree. For several weeks leading up to Christmas, my brothers and I had searched for our presents: in the back closet, in Ma and Pa's closet, everywhere. Not until we were older did we learn that Ma had hidden our presents in the icebox, which of course we rarely used during the winter months.

I found the package containing my new blue sweater and opened it. Then I found a package the size of a book. It just had to be the book I'd wished for, *Fun for Boys*. I tore it open and looked at the beautiful green, white, and brown cover filled with images of boys lifting weights, pulling rabbits out of hats, and looking upward at airplanes flying overhead. I paged through the book and read the chapter titles: "The Secrets of Cartooning," "How to Identify Aircraft (German, Japanese and U.S.)," "Building Model Planes," "How to Train Your Dog," "How to Handle a Rope Like a Cowboy," "Building a Powerful Physique," and "The Fundamentals of Jiu-Jitsu (as taught to marines, soldiers, and G-Men)." The last chapter included eight pages of recommended books for boys, including *The Deerslayer* by James Fennimore Cooper, *A Son of the Middle Border* by Wisconsin writer Hamlin Garland, *The Adventures of Tom Sawyer* and *The Adventures of Huckleberry Finn* by Mark Twain, *Adventures of Buffalo Bill* by William F. Cody, *Early Moon* by Carl Sandburg, and more. I would spend many hours in the months to come poring over this special book. (I still have it, its cover faded a bit, its pages yellowed and occasionally rolled at the edges.)

Darrel opened a package and discovered the toy he had wished for, a cash register with a little bell that dinged when the cash drawer slid open. He immediately fancied himself a storekeeper.

Donald had asked for and received a toy called a Crow Shoot. It consisted of a little cork-shooting gun and a metal fence with a lineup of crows attached. If you shot straight and the cork hit a crow, the bird tipped over. Donald, forever trying something new and often attempting something he shouldn't, quickly became bored at tipping over the little black crows. Searching for new targets for his cork gun, Donald spotted Pa sitting by the dining room stove, reading the paper and smoking a cigarette. Donald carefully took aim at the cigarette. *Pop*. The cork flew straight, and the cigarette flew from Pa's mouth. He immediately jumped and dropped his newspaper. Donald stood frozen, his cork gun in his hand, expecting the worst. For what seemed like an eternity, Pa searched for the lighted cigarette. He found it and turned to Donald. Darrel and I stood nearby, watching and waiting, curious what awful punishment our brother faced even though it was Christmas morning. Then Pa, with a smile on his face, said, "That was a pretty good shot." He picked up his newspaper and began reading once more. Donald went back to shooting at his crows. Darrel and I were certain that he had gotten away with what he had done only because it was Christmas. But we also knew he'd better not ever try it again.

At noon Ma outdid herself with a wonderful meal of baked squash, pumpkin and apple pie, canned peas and carrots, pickled beets, dill pickles, mashed potatoes heaped in a bowl with a hunk of butter melting in the middle, and at the center of it all, a beautiful roast duck. Pa preferred duck over turkey, which he said was dry and lacking in flavor.

We had come by this Christmas duck in a most interesting way. Earlier that month Darrel had participated in a raffle held at the Legion Hall in Wild Rose. He had the winning number, and one of the legionnaires handed him a gunny bag tied at the top with binder twine. Darrel didn't know what he had won until the bag began jerking and jumping and he peeked inside. It was a Muscovy duck, a big ten-pound white male with red around its bill. When he got home, he turned the duck lose in the chicken house with the laying hens. Pa thought the duck looked lonely, so he bought a couple more ducks to keep it company, and we feasted on duck that Christmas Day.

Later that afternoon, my brothers and I walked to the Davis farm, about three-quarters of a mile north of our place. Alan Davis and his adult daughter, Kathryn, lived in a ramshackle, paint-wanting house with no conveniences whatsoever. Most everyone in our community was poor in those days, but Alan and Kathryn had next to nothing—including, in Ma's judgment, often not enough to eat. Ma always baked an apple pie for them on Christmas and had us boys take it to them along with a small Christmas gift—that year a frilly handkerchief for Kathryn and a new pair of work gloves for Alan.

The Davises welcomed us in, took our coats and caps, and sat us down by the woodstove. As they opened their presents, we looked around and saw that they had no Christmas tree or decorations—no sign at all that it was Christmas.

"Tell your Ma thanks," Alan said.

"Tell her thanks for me, too," said Kathryn. As she held up the handkerchief, I saw that she had tears in her eyes.

I've never forgotten how thankful they were for the simple gifts we gave them, or their joy in having my brothers and me visit them on what must have been a lonely Christmas Day. Pa often reminded us that we all had a responsibility to look after our neighbors—especially on holidays, but every other day as well.

Fishing on Ice

During the long Christmas break from school, I had lots of time to do one of my favorite things: ice fishing. Fishing through the ice in winter differed from summer fishing in several profound ways, the most important being that it could be mighty uncomfortable if the temperatures hung around zero and a stiff northwest breeze wanted to paralyze everything it touched. Cold temperatures never deterred Pa from a day on the ice, though. He loved ice fishing even more than fishing in summer, probably because he could devote more time to it. Farmers had little time for fishing in the summer. But in winter, when you finished the chores and had enough firewood stacked behind the house, you could go cast your line.

In the years during and right after World War II, there were few cottages surrounding the lakes where we liked to fish. This was especially true of Mt. Morris Lake, one of our favorite wintertime haunts. Mt. Morris Lake, located near the village of Mt. Morris and a few miles east of Wild Rose, was only about a twenty-minute drive from our farm, depending on how slippery the roads were. When we arrived at the lake, we'd park the car alongside the road and gather up our equipment, which included an ice chisel, several tip-ups (a device for catching fish through the ice), a gaff hook (for yanking a monster fish through the hole), a bucket of minnows, and our lunch pails. My little brothers, Pa, and I would trudge through the snow until we reached the lake, then walk across its frozen surface, slipping and sliding and clutching our equipment, to a little spot at the edge of a woods where we could build a campfire.

In those days ice-fishing regulations allowed each of us to have two lines in the water at a time, so Pa chopped eight holes through the ice for our eight tip-ups. His ice chisel was a Model T Ford's rear axle that he'd had Arnold Christensen, the Wild Rose blacksmith, sharpen on one end. Arnold drilled a hole through the other end, where Pa fastened a leather thong. When chopping holes in the ice, Pa made sure to keep the leather thong wrapped around his wrist—because he never knew exactly when the chisel would punch through the ice, and he didn't want to lose it at the bottom of the frigid lake. It took Pa a while to chop all the holes; we fished for big fish—northern pike that could reach ten pounds and bigger—so he made the holes ten or twelve inches in diameter. And depending on how cold it had been so far, he would have to chop through ice that was anywhere from three inches to a foot or more thick.

When the holes were finally ready, we helped Pa set up the tip-ups. Each had a little red flag that flew up if a fish took the bait, a two- to three-inch minnow we called shiners because of their shiny sides. As we worked we discussed where we thought the big fish might be lurking, and every so often we heard a loud booming noise. "It's the lake talking to us," Pa said. The booming noise was caused by the ice on the lake contracting and forming long cracks. For the uninitiated, this booming and cracking could be quite unnerving, but for the experienced ice fisherman it was all part of the atmosphere.

With our tip-ups set, we walked back to the west shore of the lake to the little wooded spot where we would start our campfire. I gathered up an armful of dry oak branches, my brothers scrounged some dead grass, and within a few minutes a sliver of smoke rose from the little fire that we would keep going all day. A downed tree log provided a comfortable place to sit. My love for campfires began during those ice-fishing trips, when our fire dried our wet fingers from handling minnows and provided just enough heat to keep us comfortable.

About the time we arrived at the lake, other fishermen began appearing as well. Often one or more of my uncles came. Uncle Wilbur, Uncle Ed, and Uncle Fred all liked ice fishing, but they may have enjoyed telling and hearing stories even more. When the uncles had their tip-ups in place, they'd join us at our campfire and the storytelling would begin, about days when they were kids and how hard they worked, about times when the fish seemed to always bite and were considerably larger than anything we might catch today, about deer hunting and rabbit hunting, about fox and muskrat trapping—Uncle Ed was an excellent trapper and probably the best hunter in the group.

Most wild creatures either slow down or hibernate in winter, and so it is with fish. They move more slowly and feed less often. An ice fisherman spends far more time sitting and watching than pulling fish through the ice. But occasionally a story would be interrupted by a yell of "Tip-up!" when a flag announced a bite. Everyone ran to the tip-up to see whose it was—in this case, my

Uncle Fred's—and to survey the owner's technique in landing (or not) a northern pike.

Pulling a northern pike through the ice is not as easy as it might appear; it requires considerable patience and experience. The first thing to determine when arriving at the ice hole with the tip-up flag flying is whether a fish is indeed on your line, or if (a) the fish snapped at the minnow and then swam off, (b) the fish successfully grabbed the minnow without becoming hooked, or (c) it was a wind-up—meaning that the wind blew up the flag and the whole thing was a false alarm. So Uncle Fred tore off his gloves, gently reached into the icy water for the fish line, and then carefully lifted the tip-up from the hole, making sure the reel holding the extra line was free to turn if more line was needed. Sometimes the simple act of lifting the tip-up from the hole sends a fish swimming rapidly away. Uncle Fred allowed the line to play through his now icy fingers as line stripped from the reel.

At this point onlookers began offering my uncle considerable advice, most of it contradictory. "Set the hook and pull him in." "Let him have more line." Common sense usually suggests that the northern pike has grabbed the minnow and is swimming off with it before stopping, turning the minnow around, and then swallowing it, thus becoming hooked. But nobody knows for sure if this is happening, as you can't see what the fish is doing under the ice. Usually, after the first run, the experienced fisherman will wait for a minute or so and then gently pull on the line. If it goes limp, the fish is off. But more often, with the fisherman's gentle pull the northern will try for a second run. This time Uncle Fred gave the line a little jerk, called setting the hook, and then he began pulling hand over hand on the cold, wet line. He must have had a fish on the line, because the pulling wasn't easy.

As the fish approached the hole, the onlookers fell silent, all gazing at the little round opening in the ice and wondering if Uncle Fred would successfully haul out the fish. Despite the cold, beads of sweat appeared on his forehead. Not noticing how cold his hands were, he continued pulling and piling wet green fish line onto the ice, where the line froze on the spot.

"He's almost to the hole," Uncle Fred announced, and one of the onlookers stepped up with the gaff hook at the ready.

Then the fish appeared in the hole, almost filling it, its mouth wide open. With a quick motion, the assistant slipped the sharp hook into the big northern's open mouth, and it flopped out of the hole with a splash and a collective gasp from the audience.

"It's a good one," somebody said.

"Go at least six or seven pounds," somebody else announced.

With the hook and gaff hook removed from its mouth, the fish jumped wildly into the air, as high as a foot or so, trying to find its way back to the fish hole, where Uncle Fred stood ready to push it away if it should come too close to escaping back to the depths. When the jumping ceased, Fred pulled a small measuring tape from his pocket and, while a couple of men held the fish, he measured. Everyone watched to make sure the measurement was accurate—no adding an inch or two.

"Thirty inches," Uncle Fred reported, a big smile spreading across his face.

"Good fish," a grizzled old fisherman from the crowd said. "Good fish," he said again, patting Uncle Fred on the shoulder.

The crowd dispersed. With the gaff hook, Uncle Fred carried his prize toward our campfire. He stopped at the edge of the lake, where he chopped an indentation in the ice long enough to accommodate the fish. In one corner of the indentation he punched all the way through the ice to water, which immediately filled the hollowed-out spot. He placed his big fish in the hollow, where it would remain alive until he headed home later in the afternoon.

Only then did Uncle Fred return to the campfire to warm his cold hands and report exactly how he landed this big fish, from the time the tip-up flew up until the northern flopped on the ice. The story would join the repertoire of ice-fishing stories to be shared again and again, each year the fish growing a bit in length, the process of landing the creature becoming ever more challenging.

At noon we opened our lunch buckets and took out our cold sandwiches. Pa whittled a fork from a little oak limb, and we used it to toast our sandwiches over the campfire. The wood smoke added a wonderful flavor to my cheese sandwich as I sat munching and looking out over the lake toward my motionless tip-ups.

Later in the day one of my brothers caught a twenty-inch northern, and then Pa caught one about the same size. But it was Uncle Fred's big fish that made it a day I would never forget. It was a good day—but then, every day spent ice fishing is a good day, especially when the storytellers are present.

Pa and Ma made our first catch of the season into pickled fish. Here is Ma's recipe.

Pickled Fish

Clean the fish and cut it into small pieces.

Cover the fish pieces in salt water and soak for 24 hours (1 cup of salt to 1 quart of water).

Drain the fish and then soak in white vinegar for 24 hours. Drain again, saving the vinegar for brine.

In a large pot, combine fish, 2 cups of reserved vinegar with 2 cups water, 1 cup sugar, and a handful of pickling spice.

Bring to a boil. Turn fish after about a minute. Bring to a boil again and then put the fish and brine mixture in jars, add a slice of onion, and seal. The pickled fish will be ready to eat in 24 hours.

Trap Line

During Christmas vacation when I was twelve, Pa asked me if I would be interested in running a trap line along the back side of our farm. "Might catch a fox and earn a little bounty money," he said, referring to the modest fee the state paid fox hunters as an incentive to control the population of the little canids. "The pelts are worth something too," he added. Pa knew a fur buyer who would pay a few dollars for each pelt.

Of course I was interested; I always wanted to earn a little extra money, and trapping fox sounded like an easy way to do it. Besides, I was itching to use the new pair of skis I had gotten for Christmas.

Pa dug around in the pump house and found his steel traps—the kind that would spring and clamp itself around the leg of an animal unfortunate enough to step on it. He showed me how to set the trap by putting a foot on each side of the spring and then carefully lifting the plate in the center of the trap and slipping the little metal trigger in place. Setting the trigger was the most difficult and most dangerous part of the job; if your foot slipped off the spring, your finger would be caught in the trap—possibly broken—as the jaws snapped together with considerable force. Then Pa explained how to establish a set, what he called an arrangement of traps and bait intended to attract an unsuspecting fox.

On a blustery Saturday morning with a cold wind blowing out of the northwest, Pa and I skied out to the back of the farm, carrying the traps, three dead chickens, and three sizable blocks of wood from our woodpile. Pa and I always skied without using ski poles so that our hands would be free to carry a rifle, traps, or whatever else needed carrying. (We never skied just for recreation—or as Pa would have considered it, without a real purpose.)

The chickens, of course, would be bait. On occasion throughout the winter, one of the laying hens would die, and we'd toss the unfortunate bird behind the chicken house to be buried in spring, when the ground thawed. Although the birds were frozen stiff, according to Pa they would still be attractive to a hungry fox. The blocks of wood, wired to the chains on the traps, would slow down a caught animal and keep it from traveling too far in the deep snow.

We skied past our woodlot and into a field where we'd grown oats the previous summer, then stopped at the top of a little hill. "This looks a good place for a set," Pa said, pointing out several fox tracks in the snow.

We laid a chicken on the snow and then carefully set a trap on each side of it, covering the traps with a light dusting of snow. Pa smoothed the snow so it looked as if someone had merely tossed out a dead chicken, and then we set the triggers on the traps. We did all this with our gloves on, both to keep our hands from freezing and to avoid leaving human scent on the traps or anywhere around the set.

We found two additional sites and made two more sets. When we were finished, we skied back to the house. On the way Pa reminded me that I must check these traps every day, no matter how blustery or cold it got.

"Don't want a fox with its leg caught, freezing to death," Pa said. "Besides, you might snag one of the neighbor's dogs. Want to make sure you don't let a neighbor's dog freeze, or there'll be hell to pay." This was the first I was hearing about this possible problem. I wasn't looking forward to that downside of my trapping venture.

The next morning at first light, I was on my skis with my .22 in hand and on my way to my trap line. The temperature was well below zero, and the wind continued out of the northwest. When I got beyond our woodlot, the full force of the frigid wind caught me, causing my eyes to water and making it difficult to see any distance. The cold snow squeaked as I moved along, and I stopped often to turn my face out of the wind—I didn't want frostbite as a souvenir of my first day checking my trap line.

As I approached the hill, I strained my eyes to detect any movement or any sign that the first set of traps had been disturbed. If it looked suspicious, I knew I'd have to approach cautiously, my rifle at the ready. Pa had told me that sometimes an animal gets caught only by its toes and if disturbed, it will pull itself free and escape.

My eyes caught a movement. Something was there. Did I catch a fox the first night? How lucky that would be. I hoped upon hope that I hadn't caught a neighbor's dog. If I had, Pa would probably make me pull up the trap line. He didn't want trouble with the neighbors.

Carefully I skied closer to the set, my rifle ready to shoot. When I got within a few yards, the animal jumped, and I saw what I'd caught: a huge jackrabbit. The rabbit was wearing its white winter coat and had blended in well with the snow-covered field. Had the animal not moved, it would have been all but impossible to see.

I wondered aloud, "Now what am I gonna do?" I quickly saw that the trap had broken one of the jackrabbit's back legs. Worse, I knew that it was against the law to trap jackrabbits. Not only had I not caught a fox, but I had broken the law too. How would I explain all of this to Pa? Should I try to remove the jackrabbit from the trap and let it go? That would cover the legal bases, but would it be humane? How long could a jackrabbit survive in frigid weather with a broken leg? A fox or some other predator would surely find it and kill it. As I thought about what Pa would do in this situation, the big jackrabbit made another lurch, pulling hard on the trap that held its leg fast in its iron claws. Another jerk and the big rabbit would likely pull free and hobble away on three legs. I released the safety on my rifle, pulled it to my shoulder, aimed at the whiskered head with the long, black-tipped ears, and pulled the trigger. The sound of the rifle shot was muffled by the wind.

I removed the dead rabbit from the trap, covered the blood-spattered snow with fresh powder, and reset the trap. Then I headed for home, my rifle in one hand and the rabbit in the other. A few flakes of snow now flew on the northwest wind, but I scarcely felt them as I skied along, thinking about the illegal rabbit I was carrying.

"What've you got there?" Pa said when he spotted me with the jackrabbit.

I blurted out the entire story, feeling more than a little guilty about my illegal catch.

"Wasn't your fault," Pa said. "That old rabbit was nosing around where he shouldn't have been. You did the right thing by putting the animal out of its misery. Never want to let an animal suffer. If you'd let him out of the trap he would have suffered a few days before he froze to death or a fox or dog got him."

I felt better, but I wished I'd shot the rabbit while hunting. Then I could have told my friends about it. Now I had to keep quiet.

For the rest of that winter, I inspected my traps every morning, no matter how cold or how blustery the weather. I did not catch another jackrabbit. I didn't catch any foxes, either. I saw evidence that they'd come up to the sets and checked out the dead chickens, but they seemed to know that they shouldn't get too close, and they didn't.

That winter would be the first and the last time I had a trap line. When I weighed the bounty money I might earn against my chances of catching a fox plus the frigid early-morning ski trips of more than a half mile, I decided it wasn't worth it. I would have to come up with a new moneymaking venture for the winter months. I knew I could earn money the coming summer by picking cucumbers and green beans—Pa let my brothers and me keep the money we earned from picking these crops—and I knew I would earn a penny a bushel picking potatoes the following fall. But I was at a loss about how to earn money in winter. Like a lot of farmers, I never did figure that out.

Blizzard

The temperature had finally risen above zero after several days of severe cold, but when I left the house for the barn one dark January morning I noticed a few snowflakes in the air. After the morning milking, Pa glanced up from his plate of eggs, bacon, and fried potatoes and said, "Weather feels like the makings of a blizzard. Don't like the way the wind's blowing . . . switched around to the northeast overnight. And those tiny snowflakes flying on the wind—bad sign. Appears we're in for a bad one." We expected at least one big blizzard a year. And so far this winter we'd had plenty of snow, but it had come slow and easy, with little wind, and we hadn't yet been snowed in.

After breakfast my brothers and I washed up, changed into our school clothes, and pulled on our wool Mackinaw coats and wool plaid caps. Before we were out the door, Ma wrapped a wool scarf around each of our heads so just our eyes peered out: her standard frostbite preventer. By the time we left the house there were four inches of fresh snow on the ground. The wind was now blowing the snow nearly horizontal as it fell. I walked in front and my brothers walked single file behind me in my tracks. Pa had long ago instructed us that when walking in deep snow, walk in single file. “No sense more than one person breaking trail,” he’d said.

As we trekked past the Millers’ farm, I could scarcely make out their buildings through the falling snow. By this time a circle of frost had formed on the front of our scarves where our breath had frozen. The three of us must have looked like three slow-moving snowmen, as we were covered with snow from the top of our caps to the tips of our four-buckle rubber boots.

After another half-mile of trudging through the ever-deepening snow, we arrived at the schoolhouse. We stomped the snow off our boots in the entryway before entering the schoolroom, where a handful of other students were already gathered around the big wood-burning stove. It appeared a good number of students had stayed home.

In those days there was no such thing as a snow day; it was school policy to stay open no matter the weather. For many years the Chain O’ Lake schoolteacher boarded at the Jenks farm, a short hike through the woods to the schoolhouse. She usually arrived early, well before the students, to start the fire and warm the building. Even so, on days like this the schoolhouse warmed slowly thanks to cold air that sneaked into the uninsulated structure through the big windows on the north and south sides.

The ten or so of us who had braved the storm sat around the woodstove until nearly noon doing our recitations and other schoolwork. The wind rattled the windows, and I saw little piles of snow gathered on the windowsills where the wind had sent snow sifting through every crack and crevice. At midmorning recess, Miss Thompson said we must all stay inside, except for necessary trips to the outhouses. She asked me, as one of the older students, to shovel the schoolhouse steps. When I opened the outside door, it pushed aside a drift of snow three feet deep. Paths to the outhouses and to the woodshed, made earlier that morning, were already drifted nearly full.

The storm's intensity increased throughout the day. We all huddled around the woodstove to keep warm; the thermometer at the front of the room, far from the stove, read 50 degrees; even with the stove going full blast, it had not budged a degree since recess time.

At three o'clock Pa arrived to lead us home through the storm.

"How's the weather, Herm?" Miss Thompson asked.

"Not good. It's already snowed more than a foot and a half, and with the wind you can't see anything. Can't see your hand in front of your face."

"Good thing it's Friday. By Monday the roads should be clear and walking a little easier."

"Let's hope so," said Pa. "But this storm is far from over. In fact, it looks like it's just getting started."

Other fathers arrived, and as we kids bundled up in our coats and caps and scarves, they huddled briefly around the stove, warming up before starting the difficult walk home. Puddles accumulated where they stood as melting snow dripped from their heavy coats. Then we ventured out and began the mile walk home, this time with Pa breaking trail. Donald followed close behind him, and then Darrel. I brought up the rear. Pa had been right; at times the snow blew so hard that I could barely see Darrel just a few feet in front of me.

"Don't any of you guys stop walkin' without yelling first,"

Pa cautioned. "Don't want anybody lost in the storm. If you fall down, yell out, and we'll wait for you. If you fall it'll only take a few minutes for the snow to bury you."

At times I had to gasp for breath as I marched along, making sure that my little brothers were keeping up with Pa. After a quarter mile or so my chest was pounding and my legs ached. Walking in deep snow, even in someone else's tracks, is hard work. Pa kept moving, not fast, but steady, one step after the other. The snow swirled and twisted as it sifted off the tops of the snow banks the snowplow had left on either side of our narrow country road. In some places we waded through snowdrifts that were waist deep, but we kept on going. No one talked; we couldn't have heard the words over the wind, anyway.

About halfway home we stopped to rest alongside a high snow bank. We were out of the wind, but the snow kept sifting down on us. Pa checked each of us, making sure our scarves were in place with only our eyes showing. He brushed the snow from our eyelids with his big mittened hands. And then we were on our way again, step after step, step after step. I felt like I couldn't go on and needed to rest once more, but Pa kept going and my brothers—with their little legs that I know were even more tired than mine—kept trudging along behind him.

Finally, through the blowing snow I spotted our farm buildings. In another minute we were on the kitchen porch and sweeping the snow from each other before going into the house. Ma had a big kettle of vegetable soup steaming on the cookstove, and the delightful smell welcomed us in from the cold. We took off our Mackinaw coats and caps and crowded up to the warm stove, rubbing our hands together.

"Storm doesn't seem to be lettin' up," Pa said, shoving another stick of split oak wood into the hungry cookstove. "We better drag our extra milk cans down from the attic and get them cleaned up. Expect the milkman won't be coming along for a couple days, the way this storm looks."

In those days we shipped our milk in ten-gallon cans that the milkman picked up each morning and hauled to the local cheese factory. Our cows produced about four cans of milk a day, two in the morning and two in the afternoon, and we had four or five extra milk cans for emergencies such as this, enough for two days with no pickup. After two days, we'd have a problem: no place to store the milk until the milkman arrived.

Pa turned to me. "Soon as you've warmed up, grab a shovel. Lots of shoveling to do, with all this snow and wind." I shoveled a path to the chicken house first, the snow so hard I had to cut it into chunks before I could move it. As I shoveled a path to the woodpile, I couldn't see the barn, only a hundred yards away, through the blowing snow. The woodpile was a white mound; I shoveled around the bottom enough to expose some of the blocks of wood. My efforts seemed futile; as soon as I cleared an area, the wind filled it with snow once more.

I waded through the deep snow to the barn to help Pa with the afternoon chores. Snow had sifted through a crack in the barn door, forming a drift six inches deep inside, and I noticed it was sifting through the cracks around the barn windows in front of the cows as well. Frost covered the windows so thick I could peel it off with my fingernails.

With the cattle fed, Pa and I waded back through the snow to the house, dimly visible through the blowing snow. The kerosene lamp on the kitchen table, normally a beacon on a dark night, appeared no brighter than a candle through the white curtain of snow. We sat down to steaming bowls of homemade vegetable soup, thick slices of fresh baked bread, and canned peaches that Ma had brought up from the cellar. It was warm and cozy in the kitchen even though we could hear the wind tearing around the sides of the house, moaning like some wild animal in agony.

After supper Pa and I pulled on our barn coats, lit our barn lanterns, and headed out once more into the storm, which seemed even more intense than before. Again I trudged behind Pa as we carried milk cans from the pump house to the barn. The lanterns were challenged by the horizontal wall of snow, which swirled so thick around me I felt I could scarcely breathe. The cows seemed content, though, even as the snow sifted in around the windows.

With the milking finished, I crawled up the ladder to the haymow to toss down hay for the cows' evening feeding. Despite being nearly full of hay, the barn creaked and shuddered as the wind struck it full force. Snow sifted in through cracks in the barn doors and accumulated in little piles on the dried alfalfa hay that I pitched from the mows to the threshing floor and then down the hay chutes in the floor to the hungry cattle below. Normally the haymow was a quiet, peaceful place, the only sounds the coo-ooh of a pigeon or soft chirp of an English sparrow. But on this night the barn was filled with the sounds of the raging blizzard outside, every board and beam of the massive structure protesting the wind.

With the evening milking finished and the cattle given their night feed, we hauled the two cans of milk to the pump house through the still deepening snow. Back in the house we gathered with the rest of the family in the kitchen, where it was warm and pleasant, the soft glow of the kerosene lamp casting long shadows, the snap and crackle of the cookstove keeping everyone warm.

Pa reminded us of the November 11, 1940, blizzard that had blown in from the west and killed 150 people, 49 of them in Minnesota alone and 12 in Wisconsin. I had been six years old at the time. The temperature had gotten up to 60 degrees that day in parts of the Midwest before plummeting, and many duck hunters were trapped in the backwaters of the Mississippi when the storm struck. Rain turned to snow when the temperature dropped, and the wind gusted up to more than fifty miles per hour. Some snowdrifts topped eight feet.

"Doubt this storm will be as bad as that one," Pa said, "but you never know." He sat back in his chair at one end of the table and began reading a copy of *Successful Farming* magazine. Ma sat at the other end with her endless pile of socks to be darned. My brothers and I took out our homework from school, but it being a Friday evening, our hearts weren't in our studies. Every few minutes a small puff of wood smoke filtered into the room as the wind drove it back down the chimney.

"Stove's smoking again," said Ma. "Gotta do something about that, Herm."

"Wind like this, nothing much you can do," Pa replied. "Besides, a little oak smoke smells pretty good on a miserable night like this."

When we heard the clock in the dining room strike nine, Pa informed us that it was time for bed. He reminded us that we'd have lots of shoveling to do the next day. My brothers and I climbed the stairs to our upstairs bedroom, where the stovepipe from the dining room below was doing its best to take the chill from the air. A little mound of snow sat on the sill beneath a crack in one of the big east-facing windows.

We took off our outer layer of clothes, leaving on long underwear and wool socks, and crawled into bed, listening to the snow pounding against the windows and the wind tearing around the corners of our old farmhouse. It was a frightening sound, yet I knew our house was sturdy and strong and had withstood many storms such as this.

It snowed all night and was still snowing when I got up the next morning. I mushed my way to the barn, carrying my barn lantern. Pa was there ahead of me; I saw that he'd had to shovel through a drift of hard snow that came halfway to the top of the door before he could get inside.

When we finished milking and emerged from the barn, we saw just a few snowflakes flying on the brisk northwest wind. The blizzard's main force had dissipated. But thanks to the stiff wind, the drifting continued. I glanced toward Bill Miller's farm and still could see nothing but a wall of drifting snow moving across the big field south of our barn.

"Looks like no milkman today," Pa said. "Road's drifted full—and with all this wind the snow is as hard as a rock."

After breakfast we shoveled and shoveled some more. By noon we'd cleared paths to the various outbuildings and to the straw stack and the woodpile. Then we began shoveling the driveway from the road to the pump house so that when the roads were plowed the milkman could pick up our milk.

By late morning the wind had lessened and the drifting had stopped, but there was no sign of the snowplow or the milkman. Ma tried calling on the party-line telephone, but the storm must have knocked down a pole somewhere, and she couldn't get through to anyone. After our noon meal, Pa and I slipped on our skis and skied to the Millers' to see if they had any news about the plow or the milkman. Bill sat by the kitchen stove, reading the newspaper. "Nope, haven't heard a word," he said. "Phone doesn't work. Suppose we could ski down to Mac Jenks's place on County A. The county roads usually get plowed out before back roads like ours."

"We'll just wait and see," Pa replied. "Problem is the milk. You got enough extra milk cans?"

"For a couple days," Bill said, "but not much longer."

After enjoying a couple of Lorraine Miller's sugar cookies and some hot coffee, Pa and I slipped on our skis and headed back home. We skied on top of the snowdrifts that were blocking the road, five feet or deeper in places. The January sun, low on the horizon, had broken through the cloud cover, making the snow sparkle like millions of diamonds. The white snow contrasted with the brown oaks that lined both sides of our road. Wood smoke trickled from all our chimneys.

That afternoon the five of us sat around the Round Oak heater in the dining room, reading and talking about the storm. Later we filled the last of our spare milk cans. If the milkman didn't make it the next day, we'd be filling everything we could find that would hold milk.

On Sunday the road was still blocked, and we stored milk in kettles, tubs, even the washing machine. Ma skimmed cream from some of the milk and asked my brothers and me if we'd like to make butter.

I'd read in school about how the pioneers made their own butter in their kitchens, with butter churns. We didn't have a churn; we got our butter from the cheese factory where we sold our milk.

Ma poured cream in a large bowl and handed me an egg-beater. "Nothing to it," she said. "Just crank the eggbeater until you have butter."

I cranked the eggbeater's handle, slowly at first, trying to keep the cream from splattering out of the bowl. As the cream stiffened, I cranked more rapidly, and soon the bowl was filled with fluffy whipped cream.

"No butter, Ma," I said. "Got lots of whipped cream, though."

"Keep cranking," she said. "Won't be long now."

In a few minutes I could scarcely turn the handle, and then, almost as if a miracle had happened, pieces of butter appeared in the bowl, dotting the liquid that remained. I didn't believe it was butter.

"I thought butter was yellow," I said.

"It is," Ma answered, "if you make it in the spring when the cows are on fresh grass. This time of the year you've got to add food coloring if you want yellow butter."

I put a piece of my new butter in my mouth and tasted it. It didn't quite taste like butter.

"Put a little salt on it," Ma suggested.

Now the butter tasted more like the butter we got from the cheese factory. Still, I couldn't get my mind past the fact that it was white and not yellow, and somehow it tasted different to me.

As we came in from doing the evening chores on Sunday, we heard it: the roar of the snowplow slowly making its way along our drifted country road. The county had sent the biggest one it had, a diesel, to clear our road. Later we heard that even with all of its power and might, the plow struggled with the snow from this blizzard. It moved forward a few feet, backed up, took another run at a drift, and repeated the process all night long.

When we got up on Monday morning, our road was clear, a narrow path snaking through the hard-packed snowdrifts, just wide enough for the milk truck. The snowplow driver knew that it was the milk hauler that we most wanted to see. By noon that day the milk truck arrived. The milk hauler told Pa he would be making two trips, because he couldn't haul everyone's extra milk in one load. But he took all of our milk and left us some empty cans.

A day or two later, our phone service was restored. Our winter routine was back to normal. And we had another story to add to our collection of blizzard tales, one everyone in my family would tell for years to come.

Below-Zero Morning

I was awakened by the *tap, tap* of Pa gently rapping the stove poker on the stovepipe below our bedroom floor. It was my wakeup call, Pa's way of telling me it was six o'clock and time to roll out of bed, dress, and hurry out to the barn for morning milking. I wouldn't know until I glanced at the outside porch thermometer on my way to the barn that it was twenty degrees below zero.

The fire in the dining room stove usually went out around midnight, and now the upstairs bedroom was as cold as the inside of our icebox. I stuck a wool sock–covered foot out of my warm bed and thumped it a couple of times on the floor, hoping Pa would think I was up and dressing. But he had long known my ploy and tapped once more on the stovepipe, a little louder this time, letting me know there was work to do.

My brothers and I slept under piles of quilts that kept us flat and unmoving throughout the cold Wisconsin winter nights. As I crawled out from under mine, I saw thick frost covering the windows. The frost formed artistic shapes on the glass, some like giant tropical ferns, others like exotic trees with frilly limbs. To look outside and see what the weather was doing, I had to blow on the window to make a little hole through the frost. Through the gray dawn I saw nothing but snow-covered fields to the east and a slight hint of pink on the horizon, a cold sunrise on the way. It would be another bitterly cold day in the wake of a heavy snowstorm earlier that week.

I grabbed my flannel shirt and bib overalls, opened the bedroom door to an even colder upstairs hallway, and ran to the end of it and down the stairs into the dining room, where Pa had started a fire in the dining room stove. I crowded close to the woodstove as I rubbed the sleep from my eyes, put on my cold flannel shirt, and pulled up my bib overalls.

I pulled on my work shoes and walked into the kitchen, where Pa had a fire going in the kitchen cookstove. He had set the water pail on the stove to thaw the half-inch-thick crust of ice that had formed on the water overnight. The pail gently rocked on the stove, making a rattling sound as it warmed. The teakettle hadn't heated up enough yet to send forth its usual steady stream of steam. Pa had lit the kerosene lamp that sat in the middle of the kitchen table, and it sent its warm yellow light into the still frigid room. Ma was nowhere to be seen; she refused to get up until the kitchen had warmed enough so "my feet won't get cold," as she said.

I pulled on my six-buckle rubber boots, slipped into my barn jacket, pulled on my wool cap with the earflaps down, lit my barn lantern, and was off to the barn. The first exposure to twenty-below-zero air nearly took my breath away, but the air was clean and fresh, albeit lung-freezing cold. I followed the narrow path my brothers, Pa, and I had shoveled a couple of days before when the storm blew itself out. When I pulled open the barn door, I was engulfed by warm, humid air dense with the smells of cows, silage, dried hay, and manure—not unpleasant smells to a farm boy. In those days the barn was the warmest place on the farm; fourteen cows, a half dozen calves, a team of draft horses, and the herd bull created considerable heat.

I hung my barn lantern on its nail behind the cows; Pa's lantern already hung on its nail on the far end of the barn. On the little concrete walkway behind the cows stood the wheelbarrow contraption that Pa and the blacksmith in Wild Rose had invented. In it were two empty ten-gallon milk cans, one with a milk strainer stuck in its top, waiting for the first milk of the morning.

I grabbed an empty sixteen-quart milk pail and my three-legged milk stool and crawled under a cow to milk, muttering "Mornin'" to Pa. He was already busily milking one of his cows. We each had our own cows to milk, his usually the more difficult ones, those that would as soon kick your head off as look at you, plus a couple that milked hard, meaning he had to really work at it to get any milk out of them. "Cold one this morning," he said as we worked.

My cow looked around at me as I settled in as if to say, "Good morning, Jerry." I settled the stool in place, squeezed the milk pail between my knees, grabbed the front two teats, and began milking. The *zing, zing* sound of the first squirts of milk against the pail was my reward for knowing what I was doing. I thought about a neighbor who had moved into the community from Milwaukee and bought a small herd of cows that he intended to milk by hand. He had never gotten the hang of it and quickly bought a milking machine.

Soon the bottom of my pail was covered with milk, and the rich smell of fresh milk surrounded me, overpowering the ammonia odor coming from the manure gutter behind the cows. Foam began to rise from the milk as I switched from the front two teats to the back two, continuing a steady alternating pull with each hand, squeeze, release, squeeze, release, over and over and over again, until the cow was dry. About halfway through milking the first cow, the barn cats would appear, a half dozen or so of them, looking for a drink. We didn't pay much attention to the barn cats; they weren't pets, were never allowed in the house, and had just one job: keeping the mouse population under control. We did give them milk to drink; they had their own dish near the milk cans that Pa filled when he finished milking his first cow and before pouring the milk into the strainer, which was set into the top of the milk can. Other than the milk, the barn cats were on their own as far as food supply was concerned. Of course, their reward for doing their job well was a good meal.

Usually a couple of the cats couldn't wait for Pa to fill their dish. They would stand on the walkway behind where I was milking and wait for me to send a stream of milk in their direction. Although they became quite adept at catching the milk in midair, sometimes they missed and the fresh milk would splatter against the concrete walkway. Pa frowned on this practice, calling it a waste of good milk.

When the milking was finished, Pa pushed the wheelbarrow with the two full milk cans to the pump house, where he put them in the water-filled cooling tank. There they would stay until the milk hauler came, usually by midmorning, to take them to the cheese factory in Wild Rose. Well water filled the cooling tank and then ran to the outside stock tank, which was where the cattle and horses drank when Pa let them out in midmorning. Earlier that morning Pa had started the fire in the stock tank to melt the coating of ice so the animals could drink.

Back in the house I pulled off my boots, coat, and cap and washed my hands and face using warm water from the cookstove's reservoir. Ma was busy making breakfast on the cookstove, which by now was heating the kitchen comfortably. Donald and Darrel were up, dressing in front of the dining room woodstove. Soon we were all seated around the kitchen table, each in our place. On cold mornings like this, Ma often made an enormous batch of pancakes. I could eat ten of them at one sitting (Ma said I must have a hollow leg). We spread melted butter on top and sprinkled them with sugar or poured on Karo syrup or, during the war years, Ma's sorghum syrup.

After breakfast we boys changed into school clothes and then bundled up in our Mackinaws, wool caps, and mittens and scarves knit by our Grandmother Witt. As always Ma wrapped the scarves tightly around our heads to ward off frostbite. When we arrived at school our teacher would check each of us over for white areas of skin, indicating that some part of us hadn't been sufficiently covered. There we would unwind the scarves, peel off the many layers of outerwear and hang our coats and caps in the entryway, walk into the still chilly schoolroom, and settle into our desks for another day of school.

Going to Town

On winter Saturday afternoons when the roads were clear, the five of us rode to town in the Plymouth so Ma could go grocery shopping and Pa could swap stories with the local farmers who gathered around the big wood-burning stove in the back room of Hotz's hardware store.

Wild Rose, population around 550, was about four and half miles east of our farm. In winter the trip to town was often an adventure, as by January the snowplows had piled snow banks as high as six or eight feet on both sides of the now very narrow country road. If two cars met, one driver had to back up into a neighbor's driveway to let the other pass. The road's surface was snow packed and smooth, and if the wind was blowing from the west or northwest, fresh snow sifted across the tops of the big snow banks and dropped onto the road, making it difficult to see drifts the car had to plow through. When the Plymouth hit one of these drifts, the snow flew up over the hood and onto the windshield, making visibility nearly impossible as the windshield wipers struggled to clear the glass.

The car's heater, barely adequate on moderate days, failed miserably if the temperature slid below zero. My brothers and I snuggled under thick car blankets to keep warm as we motored along, usually no faster than twenty-five miles an hour. When we reached County Highway A, about a mile south of our farm, Pa turned east and picked up a little speed, as the county road was plowed wider than the back roads. The Plymouth struggled up to thirty miles an hour (in summer its top speed was fifty); any faster than that and it shook and shimmied like it might fly into pieces.

On the way to town Pa advised us, as he always did, that saving money was more important than spending it. He reminded us that Ma made much better ice cream at home than the hard-as-a-rock ice cream available at Chet Jenks's Ice Cream Parlor. He saw absolutely no need for anyone to buy brick ice cream, as he referred to the store-bought kind.

When we pulled into Wild Rose, Pa stopped at the Merc, as everyone called Arol Roberts's Mercantile, and Ma and my brothers went in to take care of the grocery shopping. Pa and I went on to the hardware store for a couple of hours of better-than-average storytelling.

Despite my father's advice, my brother Darrel always wanted to buy something on our trips to town. This particular afternoon was no exception; six-year-old Darrel had managed to convince our mother that he had to have a penny to buy gum from the machine at the Mercantile. After saying no several times, she had given in and handed him one copper penny, which would buy one stick of gum.

The gum machine was several feet tall, with four rows of single sticks of paper-wrapped gum, each one on a little tray and visible from the window at the front of the machine. With Donald watching closely, Darrel put his penny in the slot. He heard it slide into the machine—and then nothing. No gum. No penny returned. Darrel's bottom lip began quivering, but he didn't cry as he ran to our mother with the report of what had happened—or, more accurately, what hadn't happened.

Our mother, well aware of the value of a penny in the mid-1940s, stopped her shopping and returned to the uncooperative machine. What happened next would be forever imprinted in the minds of my twin brothers.

Meanwhile, Pa and I headed to the back room at Hotz's, eager to see which six or eight farmers had gathered this afternoon. As a ten-year-old I felt lucky to be the only kid among the farmers collected around the stove that day, to be joined by Dick Hotz when he wasn't waiting on a customer (which wasn't too frequent in the dead of winter). Early discussion usually centered on the war and how it was progressing, and what word anyone had gotten about Wild Rose boys who were fighting. The talk often turned to rationing and how it was affecting everyone, and who might have heard of someone selling black-market meat to relatives in the cities who never had enough ration stamps to purchase a good beef roast or some pork chops.

Before long the palaver turned to less serious topics. "Say, did you hear the one about the fellow up on the prairie?" began Walter Bowen.

"What about him?" Pa asked, knowing full well that he had become the storyteller's foil.

"Well, you remember that big snowstorm we had last week?"

"Hard to forget that storm," replied Arlin Handrich. "Still got some shoveling to do. Most of us do, I suspect."

"This fellow—some kind of traveling salesman—slid in the ditch up there on Highway 73, somewhere between Wautoma and Plainfield, one of those places where the road tends to drift a lot."

"Yeah, you don't want to be drivin' up there on 73 during a snowstorm, especially around where the Oasis Town Hall is located," said Pa.

"So what happened to the guy? He freeze to death?" asked Arlin.

"No, he didn't freeze to death."

"So what happened to him?" a farmer from east of town asked, somebody whose name I didn't know.

"Well, if you'd give me a chance, I'd tell you," said Walter, becoming exasperated at all the interruptions.

There was a moment of quiet, the only sound that of a stick of green oak wood sizzling and sputtering in the old woodstove. I sat there quietly all the while—Pa had told me that I best not say anything unless someone asked me a question—but I desperately wanted to ask, "Are you gonna tell us what happened to this guy, or not?" Still I sat, and waited, listening to the fire sputtering and smelling the half dozen different kinds of pipe tobacco the farmers were smoking. Years later I realized that it was at these gatherings that I learned how to use silence to add suspense to a story.

Walter took his corncob pipe out of his mouth and blew out a cloud of gray smoke that curled around the stovepipe, settling under the ceiling. At last he continued. "The fellow sees the light in the window of a farmhouse a quarter mile or so down the road, and he heads off in that direction, looking for a place to spend the night. The snow is deep and the walking is difficult." Walter paused once more to suck on his pipe.

"He arrives at the house, half-frozen and covered with snow. He knocks on the door, and the farmer opens it. 'Have you got a spare bed for a stranded traveler?' the fellow asks."

I was wondering if the fellow really talked that way—who says "stranded traveler," except maybe some writer in an old-timey novel?—but I followed Pa's admonition to keep my mouth closed. I was thinking that the guy's teeth were probably chattering so much that about all he could spit out was, "You got a place for me to sleep?"

"The farmer says, 'No, you aren't the only stranded traveler. All my beds are taken.'

"The traveler stands by the kitchen stove, warming his hands and wondering what to do next. Then the farmer says, 'If you don't mind, you could share a bed with a red-haired schoolteacher.'

"That comment stirs up the traveler considerably. He huffs, 'Sir, I am an upstanding Christian man!'

"The farmer says, 'So is the red-haired schoolteacher.'"

Everyone burst out laughing. They laughed so hard that Dick Hotz's lone customer looked past the sales counter to see what was going on in the back room.

Back at the Mercantile, our mother was determinedly confronting the penny-stealing gum dispenser. She gave the machine the once over, looked around to see if anyone was watching, and then wound up and whacked it. The machine sat motionless for a moment, shuddered, and then began spilling out its contents. Hundreds of pieces of gum flew out of the machine. Ma held up the bottom of her coat and began capturing the sticks of gum before they bounced onto the floor. Donald was certain that we would have enough gum to last at least a year, maybe more, and all for one penny. Darrel stood aghast, unable to comprehend his good fortune and the result of Ma's magic touch.

Once the machine had completely spent itself, the twins looked to see if it was empty. They spotted not one piece of gum on the machine's many little shelves. Ma said, "Follow me," and the three of them marched to the sales counter, Ma holding the bottom corners of her coat to keep from dropping what appeared to be a half-bushel of gum. At the counter, Ma announced, "Mr. Roberts, your gum machine appears to have a problem. Darrel put in a penny, and this is what he got."

"Oh, my gosh," said Arol Roberts. "Thank you for being so honest. Thank you!"

"Darrel invested one penny. He wants one piece of gum."

Mr. Roberts handed Darrel a piece of gum from the little mound of gum that now sat on his counter. There was no additional compensation for honesty.

"How come we didn't keep all the gum?" Darrel asked Ma later.

"Because it wouldn't be right," Ma said. And that was all she said. The case was closed.

New Ice Skates

Just when you were sure you'd figured your father out—understood how he did things and knew what to expect from him—he did something to surprise you.

By January of the year I was ten, the road past our farm had been plowed to a path so narrow that the milk truck making the daily rounds could scarcely squeeze through. The snow piled alongside the porch off our kitchen was so high a grownup would have to stand on tiptoes to peer over it and see the barn and pump house. The snow was almost too deep for sledding on the hill behind our Chain O' Lake School. The adventurous kids among us still skied down the hill, but if you tried this you had to stay in the well-worn ski track; if you strayed from it, your skis stopped abruptly and you took a header. The result was a face full of snow and an ample amount shoved down the back of your neck—not a pleasant feeling. The paths to the boys' and girls' outhouses were piled so high with snow that only the tallest kids with the longest arms could shovel them, a situation not at all appreciated by those who'd grown a bit more than the others.

One school day that January, I awakened to see that the frost that had been accumulating for weeks on the inside of our bedroom windows was melting. I saw a puddle of water on the windowsill, and when I peered outside I could see water dripping from the roof of the house. I rushed downstairs with my clothes in a bundle, dressed in front of the dining room stove, lit my lantern, and opened the kitchen door on my way to the barn. Instead of the expected blast of cold air, the air that met me was warm and moist, and the snow was mushy and melting.

"Woodpecker thaw," Pa said as I hung up my lantern and grabbed the milk pail and stool to begin milking. I never learned the origin of that phrase, but it was one folks in our neighborhood commonly used to describe a midwinter snowmelt. By the time I was sitting in my seat in school later that morning, watching the snowmelt dripping off the schoolhouse roof, I thought I saw rain falling. Recess was cut short. Even though it was warm—in the high 30s, according to the school thermometer—with the rain and the snowmelt everyone was soaked within minutes. The snow was perfect for packing, and we had hoped to build a giant snowman. But Miss Thompson called us in, saying we'd all catch pneumonia. (She often warned us about catching pneumonia, something we all feared, but I don't recall that anyone did during my years at the little country school.)

Once inside, we shed our wet outer layers and hung them around the big woodstove to dry. Most of the kids wore wool in those days—wool jackets, wool mittens, wool mufflers, wool caps. By afternoon the schoolroom smelled like a wet dog. It was a smell that no one particularly enjoyed, but we knew if we wanted dry clothes to put on at the end of the day, smelling the wool dry was the price to pay.

The woodpecker thaw and rain continued for three more days. The once formidable snow banks were rapidly disappearing. In the hollows on our farm, especially the big one in the field just to the east of our farmhouse, we began to see black smudges in the snow, and then open water as the snow melted and the water filled the hollow. The water accumulated on top of the frozen ground until the pond in the hollow was at least an acre in size, maybe larger. And then, as abruptly as it had arrived, the woodpecker thaw disappeared and temperatures skidded below zero for three days in a row. What snow was left became as hard as granite. We could walk on it, ski on it, and slide our sleds over it without breaking through.

I believe it was Pa who made the suggestion after we finished the barn chores one Saturday morning just after the hollow pond had frozen to a slippery, shimmering sheet of ice. "That pond would be good for ice skating," he said. Ice skating was one winter sport my brothers and I had never tried, for two reasons: we had no ice skates and no place to skate. Now it appeared we needed ice skates. That afternoon Pa, my brothers, and I visited Hotz's hardware store in Wild Rose.

"Say, Dick," Pa said. "You got any of those clamp-on ice skates—the kind with the little key that you use to fasten them to your shoes?"

"Herm, I think I do," Dick Hotz replied. "If I remember, they sell for fifty cents a pair. That would be a quarter apiece." Pa smiled, knowing full well that one ice skate is about as useless as one shoe, one boot, or one ski.

Mr. Hotz disappeared into the back room and soon returned carrying three pairs of brand-new, shiny silver ice skates. He handed a pair to each of us boys. I looked them over, wondering how difficult it would be to use them.

"Well, you boys better go see how those new skates work," Pa said when we'd arrived back home. "Still got a few hours of daylight."

The three of us trotted over the hard-packed snow to the pond, sat down, and fastened the skates to the bottom of our shoes with the little key that came with each pair. Soon we were out on the pond, smiling and laughing and falling—falling a lot. I soon discovered that skating was not an easy skill to learn. It took a lot of practice and a lot of trial and error to get it right. I slid my feet back and forth on the icy pond but hardly moved. I pushed off from a snow bank and quickly ended up on my back. I tried keeping one skate on the ice and pushing off with the other and immediately fell. My brothers had similar luck. Ice skating wasn't nearly as easy as sledding, which took no brains at all, and was even more difficult than skiing, which required a sense of balance. Skating required balance, strong ankles, and a sense of movement on ice that I hadn't begun to master.

At the supper table that evening, Pa asked how the skating had gone.

"Fell down a lot," I said.

"Hard to do," Donald said.

"Not easy," added Darrel.

Pa just smiled and stuffed another piece of smoked ham into his mouth.

When we got home from church the next morning, Pa asked if we planned to try ice skating again.

"Thought I might go sledding," I said. "I know how to use my sled."

"I think you should give your skates another try," he said. "I'll come down to the pond with you." I wasn't at all pleased to have him accompany us. I was sure he would stand there and laugh while we fell and fell again.

The four of us filed down the hill to the pond, and my brothers and I sat down to put on our skates.

"Mind if I try it once?" Pa asked.

"Sure," I said, but I wondered why he, an old man of forty-five, would want to try ice skating. He could fall and break something, and then we'd have more chores to do! The more I thought about this, the more I thought it was a bad idea. But I didn't say anything. Soon Pa had his six-buckle rubber boots removed and my pair of ice skates clamped onto his shoes.

"Here goes," he said, standing up and moving onto the ice. My brothers and I stood watching and wondering what we'd do if he fell and broke his arm, or his leg, or something worse.

Pa circled the pond, pushing off with one foot and then the other, smiling the whole while. Then he cross-stepped on all the turns, going faster and faster around the pond. He pulled his wool cap down to keep it from flying from his head.

My brothers and I couldn't believe what we were seeing. Pa had never said anything about knowing how to skate. He'd never mentioned ice skating when he was a kid, although come to think of it, there was a lake just down the hill from my grandfather's farmhouse.

"I hope you're watching," he said. But as I saw how easy he made skating look, I decided that learning how to ice skate by watching someone do it was akin to learning how to swim by watching a swimmer.

Soon Pa was skating backward as easily as he skated forward. And then he was cross-stepping while skating backward. What next, I wondered.

"Okay," Pa said, skidding to a stop in front of us, a shower of ice settling around his skates. He hadn't fallen once. "It's your turn," he said as he keyed loose the skates and handed them to me. We strapped our skates on again, and all three of us proceeded to stumble and fall, slip, slide, and fall again. Pa explained the importance of relaxing and feeling the motion skating required, and slowly, with his patient tutelage, we began getting the hang of it. After a week of afterschool skating, we could circle the pond without falling. Darrel caught on more quickly than Don or me; while I was still struggling to cross-step while skating forward, he was skating backward with grace and confidence.

By the end of that winter, all three of us were reasonably good skaters. But we learned a more important lesson than skating technique; we learned that there was a lot we didn't know about Pa. Now we would always wonder what he would do next to surprise us. And I would never forget how happy he was skating around our little meltwater pond like a twelve-year-old. Pa never talked much about his childhood, but I knew it had been short, because his folks had pulled him out of school when he was in fifth grade to work on the farm. He hadn't had many years to just have fun and be a kid.

Saturday Night and Sunday Morning

When I was a kid, a once-a-week bath was considered sufficient. In fact, Pa was known to say, "Too much bathing will weaken you. Saps the strength right out of your muscles." Whether that was true we never found out, for we never bathed more than once a week. And no matter the season, Saturday night was bath night.

Our bathtub, about thirty inches across and a foot or so deep, was made of silvery galvanized metal. It hung on its nail in the woodshed in all seasons of the year; during the warmer months we bathed right in the woodshed. On Saturday nights in winter, when the evening milking was done and the cows fed and bedded down for the night, Pa unhooked the bathtub from its nail in the woodshed and brought it into the house.

Pa placed the tub in front of the kitchen cookstove's open oven door, the warmest place in the house on a below-zero evening. Ma had already filled the stove's reservoir with water, and it was now warm and steaming. Now she filled the tub half full with water from the reservoir.

We each took our turn, first Darrel, then Donald, then me. We peeled off our bib overalls, shirts, and socks and stepped out of long underwear that we hadn't removed since the previous Saturday night. Into the tub we went, one at a time, with Ma responding to our shouts of "too cold" or "too warm" by adding a dipper or two of cold water from the water pail by the sink or dumping in a shot of warm water from the teakettle that steamed on the back of the stove. (The water in the tub was never replaced; Ma simply added more warm water throughout all three of our turns in the tub.)

Lifebuoy soap appeared next, a big pinkish red cake that we all used to remove the dust and grime from a week of doing chores, going to school, and all the rest that kids did in winter. Lifebuoy soap has personality. It smells of antiseptic; whether you are truly clean or not, you smell clean after you bathe with Lifebuoy soap. And everyone else knows you've bathed, as well—the smell carries like the smell of oak smoke carries on the winter wind.

After our baths we hustled off to climb into fresh, clean long underwear, shirts, overalls, and socks and were ready to start off another winter week with clean skin and the smell of Lifebuoy soap lingering for a day or two.

While we boys gathered in the dining room to play a board game or maybe Old Maid, a card game we enjoyed, Ma and Pa took their turns in the tub. When they were finished bathing and dressing, Pa carried the tub of wash water out behind the house and dumped it. He returned the tub to its nail in the woodshed while Ma toweled up the spilled water on the kitchen floor.

Often Ma and Pa would join us for a card game, usually Smear or one of Ma's favorites, Canasta. Then, when it was time for the *Barn Dance* program, Pa tuned our Philco radio to WLS, a Chicago radio station that came in well on cold winter nights.

We all stopped what we were doing and gathered around the radio to listen to the wonderful singing and storytelling. Even with temperatures well below zero and the wind whipping around our farmhouse, Saturday nights at home were cozy and comfortable.

Once a month or so, however, we ventured out on a frigid Saturday night for a neighborhood party. Everyone usually walked to these gatherings, some as far as two miles, for a chance to play cards, or dance, or just sit around and visit.

One cold Saturday night the Rapp family invited the neighbors to a party in honor of their newly wed daughter and son-in-law. Freshly scrubbed and dressed in clean clothes, we pulled on our winter coats and set out for the Rapp place, about a mile from our farm. The night was quiet save for the snow squeaking beneath our feet as we walked along the road. Moonlight created a variety of shadows on the snow-covered fields that we passed. The air was thick and clean—as clean as our Lifebuoy-scrubbed bodies. It was cold, maybe zero. But by this time in the winter we were used to the cold, and a zero-degree night was pleasant, especially when the wind wasn't blowing.

As we topped a little hill, we could see the Rapps' farmhouse ahead, the lighted windows bright spots in the dark night. And then we picked up a faint sound. Polka music. Dancing music. I noticed that both Ma and Pa were smiling when they heard the music, for now we all knew that our little community band had been invited to entertain us.

At the Rapp house, Freddy Rapp, the bride's brother, invited us in, took our heavy coats, and offered us chairs. The dining room furniture had been pushed aside to provide ample space for dancing. Our neighborhood musicians—Frank Kolka (Czech), who played the button concertina, Pinky Eserhut (German), who strummed the banjo, and Harry Banks (English), who sawed on the fiddle—sat on the far side of the dining room. Harry had lost a finger on his left hand in a haying accident, but it didn't seem to bother him a whit as he bowed his violin. There were no music stands or other such clutter (Pa told me that none of them could read music), just three farmer-musicians waiting to help us celebrate a little on this cold winter night.

I had heard them play a time or two before for birthday parties held at Chain O' Lake School, but this was the first time I had seen them at a house party. Frank Kolka tapped his foot on the floor a couple of times, and the three musicians began playing. It was wonderful music, even better than I had heard on the WLS *Barn Dance* show. Here I could see the musicians as well as hear them: Frank pushing and pulling on his concertina that had come from the old country, his big fingers flying around the buttons; Pinky (his real name was Alvin) plunking on his banjo; the mystery of Harry Banks fingering his violin with one finger missing.

They launched into the "Beer Barrel Polka," and right away folks were dancing, hopping up and down and moving around the floor to the beat of the music and smiling. These were hard times during the waning years of the Depression, and there often wasn't much to smile about. I realize now how important those neighborhood parties were for the community of farmers waiting out the long winters, and how much that little band of musicians helped everyone, young and old, put their troubles aside, embrace the fellowship of their neighbors, and have a good time, if but for one Saturday evening.

Bill and Lorraine Miller were the best dancers in the neighborhood—and they didn't mind letting us all watch them perform. They knew how to polka in double-time, their feet scarcely touching the floor as they bounced around the room. Everyone else made room for them as they whirled around.

The band shifted into an old-time waltz, which brought more people onto the floor, and then they played a schottische: *one-two-three hop, one-two-three hop, hop, hop, hop*. The room was filled with hopping schottische dancers dancing so vigorously I began to think the floor was going to collapse.

In between dances the men drank beer provided by the bride's brother, Point Special from Stevens Point, right from the bottle. A few of the women drank beer as well, but they used glasses. During lulls in the dancing, when people were gathering up enough energy to continue, they sat and listened as Frank Kolka played some of the old tunes that his family had brought from Czechoslovakia, haunting tunes that filled the room. The songs conveyed deep meaning and mystery, especially for our Czech neighbors who had family in that European country.

About eleven-thirty the music stopped, and people lined up for an enormous lunch of homemade bread, sausages of several kinds, dill pickles, chocolate cake, sugar cookies, and black coffee. The men who'd had a few beers too many laughed and talked foolish and earned wicked glances from their spouses. But there were no worries of driving with too much to drink, because everyone had walked. Besides, after walking a mile or more in below-zero temperatures, the overimbibing culprit was usually cold sober by the time he arrived home. About the only danger was crawling out of bed the next morning to milk cows with a severe headache.

At our house the next morning it was business as usual. Pa woke me up as he always did, by tapping the stove poker on the stovepipe downstairs so it would rattle in our upstairs bedroom. It was five-thirty and below zero, but the cows must be milked.

When the morning chores were done, and if the Plymouth started, we all climbed into the car and were off to church. There, sitting shoulder to shoulder with our neighbors, many of whom we'd seen dancing the schottische just hours earlier, we could still tell who had bathed the night before. The smell of Lifebuoy soap lingered many hours after our Saturday night scrubbing.

Wash Day

Winter wash days at the Apps farm often reached epic status. In theory the task was simple enough. On Monday morning before leaving for school, my brothers or I would fetch in several pails of water from the pump house and fill the copper boiler that Ma had carried in from the woodshed and placed on the hottest part of the cookstove. She waited for the water to steam just short of boiling. Meanwhile, Pa pushed the kitchen table aside and then dragged the gasoline-powered Maytag wringer washing machine and the rinse tubs in from the woodshed and organized them in the middle of the kitchen. Up to this point, everything usually had gone according to plan. A little water might have spilled on the kitchen floor and a little more dripped on the hot stove, creating a sizzle and a little steam cloud, but nothing had slowed down the process or hindered it in any meaningful way. Not yet, anyway.

Ma searched for the homemade soap, a product my Aunt Louise proudly concocted from animal fat, lye, water, and who knows what else. Her bars of yellowish brown soap were irregular in shape but uniform in their power to remove the toughest, most resistant dirt from any piece of skin or cloth the soap touched. It was strong stuff. Aunt Louise made enough soap so all the close relatives had an ample supply, usually enough for a year, and she passed out her annual gift of cleanliness at Christmastime.

With the washing machine in place—a long flexible metal tube now snaked from the gasoline engine out a crack in the kitchen door to the woodshed—Ma began dipping warm water from the copper boiler into the machine's tub, where an agitator waited to scuff the dirty farm clothes back and forth, back and forth, until they were clean.

We had no electricity and thus no electric motor to power the machine. Instead, we depended on a Briggs & Stratton gasoline engine to do the work. Briggs & Stratton, a Wisconsin company with its roots in Milwaukee, was a longstanding and well-respected manufacturer of gasoline engines. Pa had bought the washing machine based on the company's reputation. The salesman had proclaimed the little engine's virtues, from its power and sturdiness to its relative quiet—if it ever can be said that a gasoline engine, sans muffler, is quiet. However, the salesman made no mention of the ease of starting the machine, and Pa never asked about this critical characteristic.

The little black engine, neatly tucked under the white enamel washing machine, required but two controls for its operation: a kick-start lever that stuck out from underneath the washer far enough that a big masculine foot could pounce on it; and a thin, silver-colored choke wire with a small knob on its end. Starting the engine should have been simple enough: pull on the choke wire to close the little flap in the carburetor, and push down on the kick-start lever with your foot. There were no other controls to fiddle with, no other instructions to worry about.

With the machine partially filled with steaming water to give it some heft and thus keep it from leaping around the kitchen floor during the starting process, Pa pulled on the choke wire and pushed firmly down on the kick-start lever. A loud purring noise resulted. Pa repeated. More purring. Pa repeated the move again; more purring. Again and again. Ma's face wore the perplexed look she got when something wasn't going well. She had observed the saga of the starting of the washing machine more times than she wanted to recall. As the winter weeks wore on, starting the engine grew increasingly more taxing and challenging.

Pa was a man of great patience, but when his patience wore thin, it was not a pretty thing to see. His face got red, his brow furrowed, his glasses steamed up, and a fiery stream of cuss words flew out of his mouth. He called the little engine every name in the considerable vocabulary of invective that he had gained while spending many younger years working as a hired hand in a variety of jobs. For a kid like me, who was just beginning to develop a cussing vocabulary, it was an educational moment of the highest import.

After fifteen minutes of choke pulling, kick-start lever pushing, and cussing, Ma said, "Herm, the water in the machine is cooling down."

It was not the time to point out the obvious to my father, who was ready to haul the entire washing machine, its cooling water, and its nonresponsive engine to the gulley out in the back forty, to be forgotten along with other assorted junk that had accumulated there. In this darkest moment, when consensus seemed to gather that this week's washing would have to be done the old-fashioned way, with washboard and tub, the machine uttered a lonely *pop*—feeble evidence of life, but enough to give Pa new vigor and enthusiasm for the challenge at hand. The next push of the kick-start lever produced a succession of pops and an enormous cloud of stinky black smoke that poured out of the exhaust pipe and fouled the air.

"We got the bugger going!" Pa exclaimed, shifting from cussing to polite displeasure.

Ma added more hot water to the machine, its agitator now sloshing back and forth. She began shaving small pieces of Aunt Louise's homemade soap into the churning water, creating considerable foam. Soon Ma tossed in the long underwear and other less dirty clothing, such as our school clothes, socks and shirts, and her things. After each batch of clothes had an opportunity to come into contact with Aunt Louise's powerful soap and be agitated by the machine, now popping confidently along, Ma ran the clothes through the wringer and into one of the tubs of rinse water.

She finished with the filthy barn overalls. When everything had been soaped, agitated, rinsed, and run through the wringer a couple of times, Ma gathered up the basket of her hard work and marched out to the clotheslines: several wires strung between two wooden crossbars. Shoveling out the ground under the clotheslines was one of my chores, a job I did late Sunday.

On a cold winter day, especially with a stiff breeze from the northwest, the lightweight items, such as socks and shirts, dried quickly, but the long underwear and the bib overalls froze stiff. By late afternoon, Ma gathered up the dry and frozen clothes and carried them in the house to complete the drying process. She stood the frozen long underwear and the stiff big overalls around the kitchen so they would melt and eventually dry.

Upon arriving home from school on a cold Monday afternoon, my brothers and I were greeted by what appeared to be a roomful of visitors, all standing quietly around the kitchen, stiff as boards, with no heads, arms, or feet. It was something to see. I wanted to go up and ask them what they thought of winter or how they thought the war was going. By the time my chores were done and we boys had gathered around the radio for the afternoon radio sagas designed just for kids, the stiff visitors were beginning to slowly collapse, each eventually becoming a little pile of damp cloth. Ma gathered up the crumpled laundry and hung it on a folding wooden drying rack to finish drying.

After Pa finished the barn chores that afternoon, he hauled the washing machine and rinse tubs back to the woodshed. He pushed the kitchen table back in place and hung the copper boiler on its nail in the woodshed. The entire process would be repeated again the next Monday and every Monday throughout the long winter.

In spring, summer, and fall the washing machine remained in the woodshed and Ma did the washing there. The little Briggs & Stratton engine started with little effort during these warmer seasons. It obviously had no love for winter.

Box Social

With World War II finally over, the boys returned from Europe and from the South Pacific, rationing ended, electricity was on its way to the country, and farmers began buying tractors. We looked forward to a brighter future on the farm. The war years—especially the long winters of those dreadful years—had been a dreary, fearful time in our community; many of my cousins were in the service, as were several boys from neighboring farm families. Thankfully, they returned home; many Wild Rose boys did not. Little flags with gold stars in the center hung in the windows of the grieving parents.

Now people were feeling optimistic again, ready to try new things. In early winter 1945, a few months after the end of the war, Pa brought up the idea of starting a 4-H club in our community. At age ten I was eligible to belong, and in a few years my brothers could join as well. A few days later Pa stopped at the courthouse in Wautoma to discuss his idea with county agricultural agent Henry Haferbecker, who agreed to help organize a 4-H club in the Chain O' Lake community.

On a chilly late November evening, all the Chain O' Lake students ten and older and their parents gathered at the schoolhouse for an informational meeting with Mr. Haferbecker. He described the 4-H program's background and told us about some of the activities we could do as members, including forestry, soil conservation, sewing and cooking, and raising crops or calves. By the end of the meeting we had formed our very own Chain O' Lake 4-H club, complete with officers and a monthly meeting schedule. Clayton Owens, a farmer from east of Wild Rose, would be our leader and direct our activities. We even elected a club treasurer—although our treasury had not a nickel in it.

By our January meeting, we were planning what projects we would take to the Waushara County Fair in Wautoma, held each year in late August. Those of us participating in the calf project would be required to stay overnight on the fairgrounds to feed and care for our calves. Mr. Owens said that if we raised twenty dollars, we could purchase a large army surplus tent to use at the fairgrounds. Of course we were excited about the prospect of sleeping overnight at the fair and being at the center of all the activities. But how would we come up with twenty dollars, not an insignificant amount in 1945? We discussed possible money-raising activities, including asking businesspeople in Wild Rose for donations (not likely to raise the kind of money we needed) and asking our parents to chip in (they were scarcely making ends meet; they had no money to buy a tent that would be used but once a year).

Then one of the parents suggested we hold a box social. Ma explained that to put on a box social, the girls in our 4-H club and their mothers, plus any other women in the community who wanted to attend, would prepare a meal for two people, usually things that could be eaten cold, such as fried chicken, cheese sandwiches, dill pickles, and a piece of apple pie or chocolate cake. The ladies put the meal in a box—a shoe box was just about the right size—and wrapped it with tissue paper of various colors, crepe paper, satin ribbons, anything to make it stand out from the others. The more attractive the box, the higher the price it would fetch at the auction. The maker of each box was supposed to remain anonymous, but sometimes when a young lady wanted her boyfriend to bid on her box lunch, she would tell him ahead of time how she had decorated the box with the hope that he would pony up enough money to buy it.

We selected a Wednesday night in January for our box social, hoping we would be lucky and wouldn't have a major snowstorm that day. It turned out to be a cold but clear night, the kind where the air is fresh and crisp and it's pleasant to be out if one is dressed properly.

When we arrived at the school, the building was already half full, and by the time the box social was to begin it was nearly as full as the night of the Christmas program, when there was standing room only. As people arrived, the women and girls secretly added their boxes, usually carried up to this point hidden in a paper bag, to the card tables at the front of the room. It was a beautiful array of decorated boxes, most of them shoe boxes but one or two obviously cylindrical Quaker Oats boxes, all waiting to be auctioned off to the highest bidder. Even our teacher, Maxine Thompson, had made a box for the event. Her boyfriend, Orin Schleicher, was in attendance, no doubt tipped off by Miss Thompson as to which box to bid on.

Clayton Owens stood up and got everybody's attention. He told the crowd that the Chain O' Lake 4-H club was sponsoring the event, and that the money taken in would be used to buy a tent for the 4-H kids to sleep in while they were at the county fair. Next he explained the rules for the box social: the highest bidder got the box; if there was a tie bid he'd do the auction over again; the bidding was open only to men and boys; and you couldn't raise your own bid (I wondered who would want to do that, anyway).

"When a box is sold," Clayton continued, "the highest bidder should come up here and retrieve his box, and the woman or girl who prepared the box should hold up her hand, so the winner knows who prepared the meal and who he'll sit with to eat."

With that, Clayton picked up a box decorated in red, white, and blue. "What am I bid for this patriotic box?" he said in a voice that carried to the back of the room so the big bidders gathered around the woodstove could hear.

"Fifty cents," somebody near the stove called out.

"I got fifty, got fifty, who'll make it sixty? Do I hear sixty?"

"Seventy-five cents," said Bob Dudley.

Clayton looked back at the first bidder. "Make it a dollar—make it a dollar?"

The first bidder shook his head.

"Anybody a dollar, anybody a dollar, do I hear a dollar, do I hear a dollar?"

Silence.

"How about eighty cents? Do I hear eighty cents, eighty cents? I'm gonna sell it for seventy-five cents. Are you all through? Going once, going twice, sold to Bob Dudley for seventy-five cents!"

Bob Dudley came up to retrieve his purchase, looking around the room to see which woman or girl was holding up her hand. Near the front, Barbara Kolka raised her hand.

The auction continued. I won a beautifully decorated box for fifty cents. When I picked it up I learned that it had been made by Mildred Swendrzynski, a seventh grader and the treasurer of our 4-H club. If her mother had helped her with the food preparation, I was in for a treat. Mrs. Swendrzynski had a reputation for being one of the best cooks in the neighborhood.

As the bidding continued, I tried to keep track in my head how much money we were taking in. When about half the boxes had been sold, I had added up only about eight or nine dollars. We had a ways to go to make our goal.

Clayton now picked up the most elaborately decorated box of the night. He lifted it up and held it to his nose.

"Smells like apple pie in here," he said. "And I think I also caught a whiff of fried chicken." Everyone chuckled. "So, what am I bid? Who'll start the bidding at a dollar? Do I hear a dollar, a dollar?"

"A dollar," said Orin Schleicher. It seemed that the cohort by the woodstove had been waiting for Orin to open his mouth. They immediately knew he was bidding on the teacher's fancy box.

"Two dollars," came from the back of the room.

"Three," bid Orin.

"Four dollars," said another voice from near the stove.

"Five dollars," said Orin, beginning to look a little nervous.

Silence.

"Do I hear another bid, or are you through? Everybody done? I'm gonna sell it. Once, twice, three times. Sold to Mr.

Schleicher!" As Orin came up to the front of the room, Miss Thompson held up her hand. Everyone laughed.

By the end of the night we had made twenty-four dollars, enough for our tent and a bit more as well. We ended up needing the extra money to buy ropes and tent pegs. Luckily the teacher's boyfriend's bid had put us over the top.

With the bidding ended, everyone who'd purchased a box sat with the person who had prepared it. I sat with Mildred and enjoyed cold chicken and a big, delicious piece of apple pie. Of course everyone knew everyone else, so the box social was a wonderful time for chatting, catching up on family activities, and seeing how people were surviving the winter. When people filed out of the school late that evening into the cold January air, they had smiles on their faces and some new stories to tell—including a good one about how a few guys had gotten the schoolteacher's boyfriend to pay dearly for the right to eat a box lunch with his girlfriend.

Selling Potatoes

By late January or early February, Pa was keeping an eye on the price of potatoes. Many folks, especially those without sufficient storage space, sold their potato crop for a lower price in fall. But not Pa. He knew that if he was patient and waited until later in winter, potato prices would climb a bit.

Throughout the Depression and World War II, we raised about twenty acres of potatoes as a cash crop. The sandy, acid soils of western Waushara County were good for potato growing. By adding an ample amount of cow manure to the potato fields, we were able to grow a substantial crop, especially if we had sufficient rain.

Potato growing when I was growing up was essentially all hand work, except for plowing and cultivating the field, which Pa did with Frank and Charlie, our trusty Percheron draft horses. Once the twenty-acre field was plowed and smoothed—Pa selected a different field each year, to prevent potato disease and minimize weeds—he hitched the team to our horse-drawn wooden marker, which etched four little grooves, forty inches apart, in the smooth, sandy soil. The forty-inch distance between potato rows (corn rows, too) was based on the width of the back end of a draft horse—wide enough that a horse could easily move between the rows without stepping on the crop when cultivating.

In the evenings in early April, Pa, Ma, and I cut seed potatoes into little pieces for planting. Then in mid- to late April, after the danger of hard frost had passed, Pa and a hired man—often our neighbor Weston Coombes—planted the seed potatoes. They walked along the marked rows and thrust the potato planter into the ground every couple of feet to make a hole to receive the seed, and then dropped a seed potato into the planter. Pa and Weston both carried a bag of seed potatoes slung over their shoulder, reaching in for a new seed potato again and again. The potato planter made a loud "clop" when the operator pulled it from the ground and it closed. Planting potatoes, like so many jobs on the farm, could be tedious and mind numbing, until you discovered the rhythm required. Grab a piece of seed potato from the sack over your shoulder with your left hand, thrust the potato planter into the ground with your right hand. Drop the seed potato into the planter, push the planter forward so the seed goes into the ground, remove the planter from the ground, slide your right foot over the hole to cover the potato, and move on to do it over again. The *clop, clop* sounds of the planter were spaced evenly, especially when experienced potato planters like Pa and Weston Coombes were doing the job.

Potatoes do not come up quickly, sometimes taking as much as ten days to two weeks to push through the soft ground. Unfortunately, weeds are quick to germinate, so before the potatoes even emerged from the ground, Pa hitched Frank and Charlie to our sulky cultivator and cultivated the marked rows. When the potato plants finally began to appear, the never-ending hoeing began. About every week, until the potato plants had grown tall enough to shade the rows, cultivating and hoeing continued. By August the potatoes were left to mature, and usually by early September the vines began to die and dry up, leaving behind little spears of brown stems to guide the potato diggers, who began their work in October.

The second week of October, our country school closed for two weeks so all the children could pick potatoes. We called the days off from school potato vacation, but it was hardly a vacation, as we spent every day from early morning until late afternoon bent over and picking potatoes, dropping them into buckets, and then dumping the full buckets into wooden bushel crates.

Pa and Weston, each carrying a six-tine barn fork, backed their way across the long potato field, each digging two rows of potatoes as they moved rhythmically along. I followed behind, picking what amounted to four rows of potatoes at a time. Every hill of potatoes dug revealed from one to ten smooth, round, white potatoes, some as large as a man's fist, some as small as a marble. At noon we loaded the wooden crates of potatoes onto the steel-wheeled wagon pulled by Frank and Charlie, who had stood resting and waiting for us all morning. We unloaded the potatoes into the potato cellar, a small building built into the side of the hill just beyond our chicken house. The potato cellar's lower area was for the potatoes; the upper, aboveground area was used to store machinery.

After we finished our noon meal, it was back to the potato field, and the work continued, day after day, until the entire twenty acres of potatoes were safely stored in the potato cellar or in the cellar under our farmhouse. Starting with the first cold days in fall, Pa kept a fire going in the potato cellar stove to keep the potatoes from freezing. There they would wait until Pa decided the price was adequate and it was time to haul them to the warehouse. In those days several potato warehouses stood along the railroad tracks in Wild Rose; a potato buyer, eager to buy potatoes at the lowest possible price, was associated with each warehouse. The purchased potatoes would be loaded onto rail cars and shipped to Chicago and eastern cities.

In midwinter we usually enjoyed a few days of above-freezing temperatures. Pa waited patiently for these warmer days, as he knew he could not haul potatoes the four-and-a-half-mile trip to Wild Rose on a below-zero day. When he deemed the weather warm enough, he got out the bobsled, which he used in winter for hauling loads too heavy for the Plymouth to transport. For the winter Pa moved the wagon box over to the sled from the steel-wheeled wagon; at the front of the sled he placed the sleigh coupe, which looked like a little building, with four side walls, windows, and a metal roof. The window at the front of the coupe faced the team, with a slot beneath it for the leather lines that guided the horses. A little sheet-metal stove stood in one corner of the sleigh coupe, so the teamster could be comfortable as he drove the bobsled on cold days.

With the weather warm-up, Pa, Ma, my brothers, and I spent the hours after the chores were done in the potato cellar, sorting and sacking potatoes for the trip to Wild Rose. The slightly warmer temperatures outside plus the potato cellar woodstove kept us warm enough to work there for two or three hours at a time.

Pa's potato sorter was a wooden affair, hand cranked, with

a wide metal belt with holes in it. The smaller potatoes passed through the holes and fell into a potato crate; these potatoes we saved for eating. The larger ones stayed on top of the belt and then fell into huge burlap bags. As soon as a bag was filled, Pa dragged it onto the platform scale standing nearby and weighed it. He took out a few potatoes or added a few to get the weight to 150 pounds. Then he used a six-inch-long needle with a length of binder twine passed through the eye and, with a few deft strokes, sewed shut the top of the burlap bag. We sorted, sacked, and weighed potatoes until there was enough for a bobsled load, which Pa hauled to Wild Rose the next day, and continued the process for several evenings, until the weather changed again and it was too cold for hauling. Then we would wait for the next warm spell and repeat the process until the potato bins in the potato cellar and the cellar under the house were empty, save for those we kept for planting the next spring and for our family's use.

Sorting and sacking the potato crop in midwinter wasn't an easy job. But it offered a welcome break from doing the regular winter chores. And it was a task that brought the entire family together on long winter evenings, sorting potatoes, talking about how school was going, and listing to Pa spin a story or two about other years and other potato crops.

Radio

As long as I could remember, we had a radio in our farmhouse. Pa bought his first radio in the 1920s, not long after the first commercial radio station came on the air in 1922. It was a huge instrument, a battery-powered Atwater Kent that required headphones to listen to programs. By the late 1930s, Pa had replaced the Atwater Kent with a Philco table model that stood on a little table in the kitchen, near the cookstove. The Philco required both an A battery and a B battery, which were stacked under the radio and together were nearly half the size of the radio itself.

During winter the radio was my family's main source of entertainment and information about national and world events. To ensure that we had decent reception, Pa strung a wire from the back of the radio up to the second story through the hole in the ceiling where the dining room stovepipe passed, and then out an upstairs window to the top of our windmill. We had reception all right; we could pick up WTMJ in Milwaukee, of course, but also WGN and WLS in Chicago, a station in Detroit, and on some evenings stations as far east as Pittsburgh.

Until television came along a few years after World War II ended, the radio provided farm folks an important link to the rest of the world. Whereas the party-line telephone connected neighbors and allowed communication among rural towns, the radio brought the world to the farm. With a radio a farm family could enjoy the same programs city people experienced.

As a kid, listening to the radio was a privilege—you didn't just snap on the radio and twirl the dial to find something of interest. Being allowed to listen to kids' programs was used as an incentive for doing your late-afternoon chores well and promptly; you wanted to make sure that you were finished by the time your afternoon program came on the air.

We kids had plenty of choices: *Jack Armstrong*, *Sky King*, *Hopalong Cassidy*, *The Green Hornet*, *Sergeant Preston of the Yukon*, *The Lone Ranger*, *Terry and the Pirates*, *Tarzan*, *Captain Midnight*, and more. Most programs were fifteen minutes long, and the stories continued from day to day, week to week. When I finished my chores I usually had time to listen to at least two programs before supper.

Tarzan was one of my favorites. The idea of a man living in the jungle and swinging from tree to tree on long vines appealed to my brothers and me, mainly because we could mimic Tarzan by crawling up onto a beam in our barn, grabbing the thick hay-fork rope, and swinging across to the opposite beam, all the while yelling, "Tarzan of the Apps!"—pretty darn close to the real Tarzan's call of "Tarzan of the apes!"

My second favorite was *Captain Midnight*. He was one of the good guys, able to solve problems, both domestic and international, with speedy efficiency. Pretty much every red-blooded American boy tried to imitate Captain Midnight, me included. He was brave, resourceful, and clever—and he always won.

Captain Midnight's sponsor was Ovaltine, a brown concoction that came in a jar and made milk resemble something like chocolate milk. I didn't like the taste of it, but I dumped it in my milk nonetheless, because in order to receive the complete Captain Midnight story each evening, I would have to decode a message included at the end of each episode. To decode the message, I would need a decoder badge, and to obtain a decoder badge I had to send three Ovaltine labels, along with ten cents, to the Ralston Purina Company at Checkerboard Square, St. Louis, Missouri. I worked hard at drinking my Ovaltine-flavored milk, trying not to let Ma know how much I detested the stuff. Not having a decoder badge had become an embarrassment for me at school, where several of my fellow students spent time every day discussing the secret message they had heard the previous evening.

Finally I finished the second jar of Ovaltine. When Ma bought a third, I stripped the labels off all three and sent them with my dime off to St. Louis. Three days later I began looking for my badge in the mail. Two weeks later I was still looking. At last, when I arrived home from school one afternoon, I saw a little box sitting in the middle of the kitchen table. Knowing how much I was anticipating the badge's arrival, Ma had put it right where I would see it when I came through the kitchen door.

Quickly I opened the box and found the most beautiful badge I had ever seen. It was shiny gold. A dial on the top could be turned so numbers lined up with letters. It had a pin on the back so I could fasten it to my shirt. Now everyone could see that I had earned my special Captain Midnight badge. Now I could be part of the elite Captain Midnight group that met at recess each day.

I hurried to finish my chores so I could tune in to Captain Midnight. For the first time I would be able to decipher the secret message at the end. Ma didn't say anything, but I could see that she was grinning as I found paper and pencil and snapped on the Philco. The fifteen-minute program seemed to last forever as I waited for the secret message. First I had to listen to a long spiel about how great Ovaltine was and how healthy it was for those who drank it. At last the announcer said, "Make sure you have paper and pencil ready for the secret message." He began rattling off a series of numbers, which I quickly wrote down on the slip of paper.

I turned off the radio and turned to my decoder badge. The announcer had explained which numbers to line up with which letters on the badge in order to decipher today's message. I quickly did so. Then I began decoding. *What would it be? What new thing would I learn that only those with decoder badges had the opportunity to see?* I was so nervous that my hands shook as I wrote down the letters corresponding to the numbers the announcer had given me.

T-R-O-U-B-L-E A-H-E-A-D

It certainly was not an earth-shaking message. As I learned after a few more evenings of deciphering secret messages, they usually were a briefest-of-brief preview of the next episode—and often abundantly obvious. There was always trouble ahead, that's what made the program interesting! Even worse, about once a week the secret message turned out to be an advertisement for Ovaltine, which I didn't appreciate one bit. I hated Ovaltine.

The next time Ma asked me if she should buy more Ovaltine, I replied, "No. Buy Wheaties." Wheaties sponsored *Jack Armstrong*, and I was switching my allegiance to "the All American Boy," which was how Jack Armstrong was described by the program announcer.

In addition to the late-afternoon programs designed especially for the children, our entire family listened to an array of evening programs, including the comedies *Amos and Andy*, *Fred Allen*, *Bob Hope*, *Jack Benny and Mary Livingston*, *Red Skelton*, *Lum and Abner*, *The Aldrich Family*, *Edgar Bergin and Charlie McCarthy*, *The Great Gildersleeve*, *The Life of Riley*, and *Fibber McGee and Molly*. I loved Fibber and Molly's famous cluttered closet, with its mounds of stuff that came pouring out whenever the door was opened. I thought everyone must have a closet like that.

We also enjoyed the music shows, such as *Kraft Music Hall*, *Guy Lombardo Show*, and *Your Hit Parade*, and every Saturday night we made sure to tune in the WLS *Barn Dance*, broadcast from the Eighth Street Theater in downtown Chicago. Our toes tapped to the guitar picking and banjo strumming. The performers—Lulu Belle and Scotty, Red Blanchard (born in Pittsville, Wisconsin), Arkie the Arkansas Woodchopper, Pat Buttram, and many others—were transported to our kitchen on Saturday nights.

We listened to variety shows, too, like *Arthur Godfrey's Talent Scouts*, *The Ed Sullivan Show*, and *Major Bowes' Original Amateur Show*. Ma sometimes took in the radio soap operas broadcast during the day, including *Ma Perkins*, *Our Gal Sunday*, *Stella Dallas*, *Backstage Wife*, and *The Romance of Helen Trent* (". . . because a woman is thirty-five or older, romance in life need not be over").

On long winter nights we also enjoyed dramas such as *The Shadow* ("the Shadow knows"), *Inner Sanctum* with its squeaking door, *The FBI in Peace and War, Gang Busters*, and *Death Valley Days*. Pa liked listening to the Friday night fights: Joe Louis and Max Schmelling, Jack Dempsey and Gene Tunney. One time when our radio battery died on a Friday, Pa walked to Bill Miller's farm on a below-zero night to listen to the fights on the Millers' radio.

Pa listened to the weather and farm markets every day at noon, and Pa and Ma listened to the news programs every evening, particularly those hosted by A. V. Kaltenborn (who was born in Milwaukee and grew up in Merrill, Wisconsin), Lowell Thomas, and Gabriel Heatter.

We even listened to the radio at our country school, tuning in to programs broadcast by the University of Wisconsin in Madison on radio station WHA and, for central Wisconsin, WLBL. I especially loved the weekly nature program hosted by Ranger Mac, Professor Wakelin McNeil from the University of Wisconsin College of Agriculture and state 4-H leader. James Schwalbach offered *Let's Draw*, helping us make interesting pieces of art at our desks while we listened to Schwalbach's directions broadcast from a hundred miles away. And Professor Edgar "Pop" Gordon's show *Let's Sing* taught us to appreciate music as we attempted to sing along.

Both at school and at home, the radio entertained us, informed us, and made the winter days more bearable. The old Philco was much more than a source of news and entertainment; it was a member of our family.

Lamps and Lanterns

One of my most pleasant memories is sitting around the dining room table on a cold winter night, the only sounds the quiet hiss of the Aladdin lamp that sat in the middle of the table and the occasional crackling and snapping of the fire burning in the stove. My father was at his place at the end of the table, reading the daily paper (a day late, as the *Milwaukee Sentinel* came by mail). My mother sat at the other end of the table, patching the never-ending holes in our bib overalls. My brothers and I worked on our homework, solving arithmetic problems, studying maps for geography, or finishing a book report.

For most of my childhood, the only indoor light I knew was that made by a kerosene lamp or lantern. We had two kerosene lamps in the kitchen, one that sat in the middle of the kitchen table from late October until early April and another that hung on the east wall of the kitchen near the door to the dining room. That one had a shiny reflector behind it, designed to throw the light back into the room. The only time Ma moved the lamps was when she filled them with kerosene, which Pa bought in Wild Rose at Hotz's hardware store and kept in the woodshed in a one-gallon can—enough kerosene to last at least a week for both our lanterns and lamps. The cost of lighting our house and barn was minimal; kerosene was about fifteen cents a gallon at Hotz's.

In the dining room an Aladdin lamp always stood at the center of the table. Although it too burned kerosene, it produced twice as much light as the kerosene wick lamp in the kitchen. Similar to a gasoline lantern, the Aladdin lamp had no wick and instead had a mantle, a fragile little piece of clothlike material that glowed brightly when the lamp was lit. For reading, mending, and other close work, we sat at the dining room table where the light was brightest.

I had my own bedroom lamp, a small kerosene lamp with a carrying handle. It had been my grandmother's, and I was cautioned to take good care of it and be very careful not to drop it. Of course, dropping it would do more than break the lamp; a dropped lighted lamp was likely to set the house on fire. And while a house fire anytime is a disaster, a house fire in winter is a catastrophe. When my brothers and I went to bed on a winter evening, I hooked my index finger through the lamp's handle and led the way. The little lamp provided all the light we needed to make our way up the steep stairway and along the frigid hallway to our bedroom. I set the lamp on the dresser while we undressed for bed—the rule was, the last one in bed blew out the light.

This rule was followed downstairs as well. The last one out of a room blew out the lamp or, in the case of the Aladdin lamp, turned off the kerosene supply. When my children, who had always known electricity, were small, I often caught myself saying, "Blow out the light when you leave your room." Their response was always, "Huh?"

Pa and I each had our own kerosene barn lantern, the kind

with a wire-protected globe and a heavy wire handle that you could hang on a nail behind the cows. When Pa hung his lantern at one end of the barn and I hung mine at the other end, they provided enough light for us to milk cows by hand on dark winter mornings and evenings—but just barely enough, as many corners of the barn remained dark or in deep shadows. Having a considerable imagination, I pictured all kinds of interesting things happening in the dark corners where the dim lantern light never reached. I imagined creatures mythical and real that I had read about in school lurking there: ghosts and ghostlike apparitions, dragons, wild animals of ferocious dimensions, and more.

A few years ago, I was giving a school talk about what it was like on the farm when I was a kid. I told the children that my brothers and I did our homework by lamplight. A fourth grader held up his hand with a serious, quizzical look on his face. "Mr. Apps," he began, "if you didn't have electricity, how did you watch television?"

I explained that television hadn't yet made its way to Wisconsin when I was a boy, and even if it had, we had no electricity at our farm to power a TV. Of course, that changed in 1947. By spring of that year we had electricity on our farm, and electric lightbulbs illuminated the rooms of the house with a brightness we had never known—and exposed the dust that we hadn't realized was there. My mother, a fastidious housekeeper, cleaned for a week after electric lights arrived.

The shift from lamps and lanterns to electric power had a profound effect on my family. Several of my friends had gotten electricity at home long before we did; now I would no longer be embarrassed to invite friends over or hold a 4-H club meeting at my house. And Ma need not be ashamed to have her fussy city relatives visit. Before long an electric motor powered Ma's washing machine, another pumped water, and still another ran a milking machine in the barn. In a matter of a few months, electricity had changed our lives irrevocably, and lamps and lanterns became symbols for our pre-electricity days on the farm.

Perhaps most significantly, electricity shortened the long, dark nights of winter. Now we walked to the barn for morning and afternoon chores with a yard light showing us the way. I no longer had to carry a lantern into the haymow so I could see to toss down hay; with a simple flip of a switch, the haymow was nearly as bright as a summer day.

But there were downsides to progress. Now we could sit anywhere in the kitchen or dining room to do our work, as the light was ample in both rooms. But I missed having family close, gathering at the dining room table as we had always done when lamps and lanterns lighted our lives.

Neither of my parents ever became quite comfortable with electricity. They kept the kerosene lamps and barn lanterns handy; when the power went out, as it did on occasion—often during storms, but sometimes for no apparent reason—the old standby light sources were ready. With the arrival of electricity to the farm, we gave up some of our self-sufficiency, something my father always considered extremely important. Now we depended on someone else to provide a basic need. It was one of the trade-offs we made when we shifted from simplicity to, as my mother sometimes called it, "that newfangled electricity."

Signs of Spring

I'd heard it often said by Pa, and by my teacher as well: "March comes in like a lion and goes out like a lamb." It was almost always true. Early March usually looked a whole lot like February, with plenty of snow and cold, though not extreme cold. (Ten-below-zero days were rare in March, but not unheard of.) And by the end of the month, the days were becoming noticeably longer and the sunlight felt warmer.

Somewhere around mid-March, when I had had about as much winter as I could stand, when I was thoroughly tired of shoveling paths to and from our various farm buildings, and when skiing and sliding down a hill had lost almost all of its appeal, I woke up one morning and saw from my bedroom window snowmelt dripping from the roof. It was evidence of the first major thaw, the first shrinking of the snowpack since that brief "woodpecker thaw" back in January or February. As I walked out to the barn, the snow was mushy underfoot, and I could smell spring. Hard to describe but distinctive, the smell of spring comes on a gentle southerly breeze that washes over the tired old snow banks. It trickles upward from the melting snow, a tantalizing and optimistic smell of warmer days to come.

The barn animals sensed the first hint of spring in the air, too. After we finished the milking, Pa let the milk cows and the calves out into the barnyard. They were the most foolish-acting bunch of long-cooped-up animals I'd ever seen. They ran with their tails in the air, jumping up and down in the mushy snow. They feinted fighting with each other, butting heads, backing off, and doing it again, not for real, just for play. With the barn doors wide open, the stuffy odors transformed into a fresh smell. Pa was smiling. I was smiling. I think the animals were smiling, too. It was time for a seasonal change.

Later that morning the phone rang. It was George Collum, the depot agent in Wild Rose, calling. "Your baby chicks are here," he said. "Pick them up as soon as you can."

Back in February we had ordered a hundred or so white leghorn chicks from a hatchery in southern Wisconsin, enough to replace the laying hens that had passed their prime and were on their way toward becoming chicken soup. We also ordered twenty-five White Rock chicks to raise for selling and eating. Now the whole peeping bunch had arrived on the morning train.

Wild Rose's depot was a little one-story building along the Chicago and Northwestern Railroad tracks that featured a small office for the agent, a larger waiting room for passengers, and an equally large, unheated baggage room at the back of the building. The moment we opened the door to the waiting room, we could hear the peeping of hundreds of baby chicks piled in cardboard boxes. Several other farmers' chick orders had arrived along with ours. Mr. Collum helped us find our two boxes, Pa signed a paper, and we loaded the chicks in the back of the Plymouth. The peeping continued all the way home.

A small building to the west of the straw stack served as our brooder house, where we housed the little chicks until they were large enough to become part of the laying flock (the leghorns) or heavy enough for butchering (the White Rocks). The brooder house would need a good cleaning before it was ready for the chicks, a job we'd tackle as soon as we dropped the chicks in the house. We toted the two boxes into the house and put them in a warm, cozy spot near the cookstove. There they would continue peeping throughout the rest of the day and all night.

We swept out the brooder house, started the brooder stove (which burned coal and thus held the heat longer than a woodstove), and gathered up the long, narrow feeding trays from where they were stored and some quart jars to make into chick waterers. We cleaned and washed everything thoroughly; chicks easily succumb to any disease that might have overwintered in the feeding and watering equipment.

The next day we carried the little chicks to their new quarters in the spruced-up brooder house. They scampered about, ran into each other, fell over, found the watering jar, found the feeder, and eventually found their way under the big hood of the brooder stove, where they would be warm. They ceased peeping, for the most part. Pa and I stood watching them for some time; little animals, no matter what kind, are a joy to watch, and chicks are especially entertaining, with their skinny yellow legs, tiny feet, and fluffy, soft yellow coats.

The next day one of our sows gave birth to a litter of pigs, ten squirmy little packages of wrinkled pink skin and endless appetites. We made sure there was plenty of straw in the hog house so the little pigs would stay warm. A couple of days later, as the warm temperatures continued and the snow melted enough so we could see the brown hilltops once more, I heard the first flock of geese winging north, calling loudly to each other and to us—announcing with clear tones that spring indeed was on the way.

In most years by mid-March, a little stream of meltwater trickled from behind the corn crib, continued on between the house and the barn, and finally curled under the barnyard gate to disperse in the barnyard. One year Pa cut two pieces out of a cedar shingle, notched them, and pushed them together to fashion a little waterwheel with four paddles. With two other pieces of shingle wood he made a little frame. He placed his contraption in the meltwater river.

In early morning when the temperature had fallen below freezing, the little waterwheel hung motionless in its frame, but usually by midday, with climbing temperatures and more snow melting, the waterwheel turned furiously, making a *flip, flip* sound. The waterwheel turned for more than a week; as we went about doing our spring chores, Pa, my brothers, and I would stop occasionally to watch and listen to it. One warm late afternoon, we noticed that the meltwater river had stopped running and the water wheel no longer turned. On that day we knew that spring had truly arrived. Now it was time to remove the banking from the sides of the house and look forward to a week of muddy, sometimes nearly impassable roads and the first green grass springing up on the south side of the house.

Winter was over. Spring was here. And with spring came another round of farmwork that would continue nonstop until the first snowflakes appeared in the fall. Although Pa didn't say it in so many words, almost of all of what we did on the farm was preparing for winter. With the coming of spring, the cycle of the seasons began once more.

Remembering

Many winters have come and gone since those days I spent growing up on the farm. Although these stories happened many years ago, the details are as vivid to me as if I experienced them yesterday.

I remember the feeling of walking back to the house after the evening milking on a below-zero night. I would look upward and behold a sky full of stars, for there was no light pollution, nothing to block out the tiny slivers of light punching holes in the black night.

I remember trees in winter, the oaks and maples, aspens and birch, stark, thick gray trunks and bare branches like hundreds of skinny fingers reaching skyward, grasping for the unknown, embracing winter and allowing it to paint ribbons of snow on their branches. Evergreens became pieces of art: the spruces tall and pyramidal, covered with snow from top to bottom; the red and white pines looking a bit tortured as their limbs sagged under the weight of the winter white (indeed, some lost their limbs to the heavy weight—one of nature's ways of pruning).

I have always been intrigued by snowflakes, especially the

large, cottonlike ones. I like to watch snowflakes falling en masse, and I marvel at how quickly they can turn a drab and brown landscape into a world of white. Most impressive to me is a close-up study of a single snowflake: a frilly, fragile piece of frozen water that nature has arranged into the most intricate of patterns. It's claimed that no two are alike, but that seems nearly impossible when millions and billions of snowflakes fall in a single storm. On a cold day I might study a single snowflake for a minute or two, examining its elaborate pattern and comparing nature's work with my Aunt Louise's delicately crocheted doilies. But if the temperature is near freezing, the little snowflake caught on my sleeve allows me only the briefest glimpse before it melts into a tiny drop of moisture. With all of the intricate beauty nature creates in a single snowflake, it seems a waste that this artistic creation exists for only a few seconds.

Winter brings sounds heard only during those cold months. A crow's call in winter is one of my favorite sounds. Crows are tough birds. Songbirds pack up and leave for the south in winter. So do wild ducks and Canada geese and sandhill cranes. But not the crows. On a cold day when I'm out walking, I often hear crows calling, a lonesome, solitary sound. When I hear it I am reassured; winter may be the harshest season, but the crows remain, withstanding the worst that nature throws at them.

Perhaps the most striking and impressive sound of winter is the sound of silence. In winter the birdsong and animal chattering and fluttering of leaves has ceased; on a windless day, there is often no sound at all. As a kid I often went on dark and cloudy days to the woodlot behind our house, on skis if the snow was deep, on foot if it was not. I usually carried my .22 rifle, but

I wasn't interested in hunting. I would stop moving and simply listen to the quiet of winter. In a world of noise, profound silence can be jarring. Even then I was straining to hear sounds—a crow calling in the distance, a breeze moving through the tops of the bare oaks. But there was no sound except for my own breathing. Such an experience takes getting used to. I may not have understood the power of silence in those days, but I do today, when it is more difficult to find than it was when I was a kid.

Some sounds of winter can be downright unnerving. Young black oak trees do not drop their dead leaves in fall like their more mature relatives do. The dead leaves cling to their branches, and when the winter winds blow, the dry, brown leaves rattle, a deathly sound on an otherwise quiet day. The moaning of the winter wind pushing through the bare tree tops on a dark winter's eve is ominous, too, reminding me of Halloween, when mysterious creatures of the night move about, preying on the unknowing.

I remember so well the smells of winter: the tangy smell of the corn silage we fed to our cows; the earthy smell of ground corn and oats; the slightly musty smell of dried hay, alfalfa, and clover; the bright summer smell of the oat straw we carried from the straw stack behind our barn to bed the cows. The smells all tangled together when you entered our barn in winter, punctuated by the odor of cow manure. As Pa and I milked cows, the myriad barn smells mixed with the aroma of fresh milk.

The most pleasant smell of all was that of oak smoke trickling from our two farmhouse chimneys. Walking home from school on a cold afternoon, I often smelled oak smoke before I could see our house, a promise that I would soon be warm again.

Winter is a time for stories, and I remember so many of them; stories that range from preparing for winter to enduring the depths of the season to welcoming the first hints of spring. Just as I looked forward to the coming of winter with its change of pace, its moments of silence and calm, I looked forward to the coming of spring, the frantic, never-ending work of summer, and the fall harvest. Such is the joy of living in the North, where the seasons are distinctive, each one anticipated, each one relished.

Of all the seasons, winter is the most striking and most influential on the lives of people who experience it. It is not merely the length of our winter that creates the band of people called "northerners." It is the less tangible, often even mythical characteristics of winter that forge a true northerner. For winter is more than cold and snow, frozen water pipes, slippery roads, and dark and dreary days.

Winter is

a quiet season, when nature rests:
the trees and the grasses,
the wildflowers and the birds,
the animals and the pond creatures.
Winter is a time for endings and a time for beginnings.
A time to regroup and a time to reconsider.
A time to reflect and a time to revise.
A time to evaluate and a time to plan for the morrow.

Winter is a season of great beauty,
blacks and whites and grays
and a sprinkling of green from the pines,
the firs and the spruces that dot the northern regions.
Winter is a season of subtle shapes with few sharp edges
as snow blankets the land with a soft and curving cover.
Winter is a season of subtle sounds:
the almost imperceptible sound of snowflakes falling,
the rustling of bare tree branches caressed by a winter breeze,
the quiet dripping of meltwater from a farmhouse roof.
Winter is a time to listen for the silence,
when the cold tightens its grip,
turning breath into clouds and thickening the ice on the lakes,
when snow cover muffles all sound.
Winter is like a great river,
always the same but constantly changing,
each winter resembling the one before,
but each like no other.
Winter is a season that demands respect,
insists on it.
It is a season that refuses to be ignored.
Winter is a season that never leaves us.
It is forever a part of who we are,
what we believe and value,
and how we see the world.

Acknowledgments

My twin brothers, Donald and Darrel, helped me recall many of the stories I've included in this book. Occasionally we didn't agree on some of the details—a good reason to have just two siblings, as you can go with a vote of two out of three when disagreement occurs. A case in point: in the Thanksgiving story, Darrel insists that the dog in the story was named Sport. Donald and I remember him as Ralph.

As is true of all my books, my wife, Ruth, read every word of every chapter and made many suggestions for improvement. And of course Kate Thompson, with an eagle eye, ferreted out every last error, pushed me to explain when I assumed people would know something (everyone knows a .22 rifle is illegal for deer hunting, right?), and generally made my sometimes clunky prose readable. A big thank-you to all.

ABOUT THE AUTHOR

Photo by Steve Apps

Jerry Apps was born and raised on a central Wisconsin farm before electricity, indoor plumbing, and central heating came to the country. From first through eighth grade he attended a one-room country school. And he experienced many winters on the farm.

He is a former county extension agent and professor emeritus from the College of Agriculture and Life Sciences at the University of Wisconsin–Madison, where he taught for thirty years. Today he works as a rural historian, full-time writer, and creative writing instructor.

Apps has published more than thirty nonfiction, fiction, and children's books with topics ranging from barns, one-room schools, cranberries, cucumbers, cheese factories, and humor to farming with horses and the Ringling Brothers Circus. He has written about billy goats, farm dogs, barn cats, country boy pranks, early farm tractors, and Fourth of July celebrations.